The Father of Love

The Father of Love

Janette Oke

BETHANY HOUSE PUBLISHERS
MINNEAPOLIS, MINNESOTA 55438
A Division of Bethany Fellowship, Inc.

242   UQJA
OKE

Editorial development by Blue Water Ink,
Grand Rapids, Michigan.

Artwork by Roselyn B. Danner.

Copyright © 1989
All Rights Reserved

Published by Bethany House Publishers
A Ministry of Bethany Fellowship, Inc.
6820 Auto Club Road, Minneapolis, Minnesota 55438

Printed in the United States of America

Library of Congress Cataloging-in-Publication Data

Oke, Janette, 1935–
     The father of love / Janette Oke.
          p.   cm.
     Excerpts from the Love comes softly series.
     1. Devotional calendars. I. Oke, Janette, 1935–
Love comes softly series. II. Title.
BV4811.044   1989
242—dc20   89–27350
ISBN 1-55661-064-5   CIP

FOREWORD

Dear Readers,

Prior to publication of *Love Comes Softly* in 1979, when I had sat down at my typewriter to begin the journey with Clark and Marty, I had no idea that we would travel with them for such a long time and through two more generations. They have become dear friends—and I will miss them.

My initial purpose in writing Christian fiction was to help to provide an alternate choice of reading material for those who enjoy novels. I had found that many of the selections on the general bookstore shelves were not pleasing to me as a Christian. Nor did I want my children or grandchildren to be limited to this type of material.

Thus *Love Comes Softly* was written in the hope that our readers might enjoy a simple story that also was uplifting.

Through the eight novels in the Love Comes Softly Series, Marty and Clark moved into old age—but unlike us they need never fail in health or lose their vitality. To us they may ever be young, continuing to teach simple lessons by their deep personal faith in a constant God and their simple, yet moral way of life.

Though we now go on to other things, I do hope that you, like me, will return for a brief visit with them now and again.

God bless,
Janette Oke

CONTENTS

LOVE COMES

SOFTLY

GRIEF

"Oh, Clem, what'll I do?" Marty sobbed until she had no more tears. The digging continued, and the scraping of the shovels lay bare her heart. Time stretched on. She realized that other neighbors were arriving. She must pull herself together. Clem would be ashamed of her.

She climbed from the blankets, slipped out of the wagon, and walked down to the spring to wash away her tears and straighten her tangled hair. Then she squared her shoulders, lifted her chin, and went back to meet her new neighbors.

There was a kindness in all of them. She could feel it. It was not a piteous thing, but an understanding. This was the West. Things were hard out here. Most likely every neighbor there had had a similar time, but you didn't go under—you mustn't; you must go on. There was no time nor energy for pity here—not for self, not for one another. It took your whole being to face what must be faced. Death, too, must be accepted as part of life, and though it was hard, one carried on.

The visiting preacher spoke the words of commitment. He also spoke to the sorrowing—one lone, small person, the widow of the deceased; for one could hardly count the baby she was carrying as one of the mourners.   [13–14]

Grief is a natural and healthy emotion when a
loved one dies, but self-pity helps no one.
*Though he cause grief, yet will he have compassion according
to the multitude of his mercies.*
LAMENTATIONS 3:32

Marty had no money to stay in town, not even for one night, and no hope of getting any. What kind of a job could she get? What future did she have? Her feet carried her to the wagon, though she wanted to crawl away and let the world cave in on her. Her senses played tricks on her, making her wonder what was real and what imagined.

"Ma'am." The closeness of the voice startled her.

A man stood before her, cap in hand. Her eyes looked to him, but her lips refused to answer his address.

"Ma'am, I know thet this be untimely—ya jest havin' buried yer husband an' all—but I'm afraid the matter can't wait none fer a proper-like time an' place. My name be Clark Davis, an' it peers to me thet you an' me be in need of one another. It jest be a matter of common sense. Ya lost yer man, an' are here alone. Ain't no wagon train fer the East 'til next spring. Me, now, I have a little 'un, not much more'n a mite—an' she be needin' a mama. Now as I see it, if we marries we could solve both these problems. The preacher is only here fer today an' won't be back through agin 'til next April or May, so's it has to be today. I know," he stammered, responding to the horror in Marty's eyes, "it don't seem likely, but what else be there?" [15–16]

Though it goes against our senses to think so, what seems to be a bad alternative may be the best one.

Return thou . . . and Ruth said, . . . Whither thou goest, I will go.
RUTH 1:16

CHOICES

Clark turned and strode away. The sag of his shoulders told Marty how much the words had cost him. Still, she thought angrily, what kind of a man could propose marriage to a woman who had just turned from her husband's grave? Despair welled within her. I'd rather die, she told herself. I'd rather die. But what of Clem's baby? She didn't want death for him, for her sake or for Clem's. What a position to be in. No one, nothing, out in this godforsaken west country. Family and friends were out of reach and she was completely alone. She knew that he was right. She needed him and she hated him for it.

"I hate this country! I hate it! I hate him, the cold miserable man! I hate him! I hate him!" But even as she stormed against him, she knew that she had no out.

She wiped her tears and got up from the shady grass. She wouldn't wait for him to come back in his lordly fashion for her decision. She went into the wagon and began to pack the few things that she called hers.   [17]

Giving in to what may be unpleasant is better than
giving up hope.
*For to him that is joined to all the living there is hope: for a living dog
is better than a dead lion.*
ECCLESIASTES 9:4

SENSITIVITY

Clark and Marty rode in silence in his wagon. The preacher was at the Graham's. Clark's daughter, Missie, was there, too. Marty sat stiff and mute as the wagon jostled on. She lifted a half-dead hand to push hair back from her hot face. Clark looked at her with concern in his eyes.

She was relieved to see the homestead of the Graham's appear at the base of a cluster of small hills, but she noticed nothing of her surroundings. In what seemed almost an immoral shortness of time she was hearing the familiar words. She must have uttered her own response at the proper times, for the preacher's words came through the haze . . . "I now pronounce you man and wife."

After eating a meal she did not taste or later remember, Marty walked out with Mrs. Graham. There were no congratulations or well-wishing. No one tried to make an occasion of the wedding, and Marty was grateful for that. One misplaced word, no matter how sincerely spoken, would have broken her reserve and caused the tears to flow. But none had been spoken. Indeed, the marriage was not even mentioned. These pioneer people were sensitive to the feelings of others.

[18–20]

The most sensitive response may be silence.
He that refraineth his lips is wise.
PROVERBS 10:19

RELIGION

Marty cried herself to sleep that afternoon and didn't awaken until dusk. Aware of someone stirring in the kitchen, she smoothed her wrinkled dress and headed toward the smell of coffee. Clark motioned her to a chair at the table.

"I'm not much of a cook," he said, "but it be fillin'."

Just as Marty was about to help herself to a pancake, she was stopped short by Clark's voice. "Father, thank ya fer this food ya provide by yer goodness. Be with this, yer child, as Comforter in this hour, an' bless this house an' make it a home to each one as dwells here. Amen."

Marty had heard of people who had a God outside of church, but she had never rubbed elbows with one before. Nor did she wish to now. What good did his God do him? He still needed someone to help with his Missie. Oh, well, if she remembered right, people who had a God didn't hold to drinkin' an' beatin' their women. Maybe she wouldn't have to put up with that. A new wave of despair overwhelmed her. She knew nothing about this man. He could be anything! Maybe she should be glad he was religious. It might save her a heap of trouble.   [23–24]

Being religious doesn't always save us "a heap of
trouble," but it ought to keep us from causing
trouble for others.

*Pure religion and undefiled before God and the Father is this, to visit
the . . . widows.*
JAMES 1:27

COMPASSION

Marty took a deep breath and stooped to scoop up Missie, who reacted immediately with screams like a wounded thing, kicking and lashing out as she was carried away. Marty deposited her on the bed and was shocked to hear Missie clearly and firmly state between screams, "I—wan'—Mama."

So she did remember. Marty's anger began to melt. Maybe Missie felt about her the way she did about Clark—angry and frustrated. She didn't really blame her for crying and kicking. She would be tempted to try it herself had not life already taught her how futile it would be.

Missie looked so tiny and helpless. Marty realized that here was a person, at less than two years of age, that life had already hurt. What deserving thing had this little one done to have the mother she loved taken from her? Marty's own baby stirred within her. She placed a hand on the spot that was slowly swelling. Again she looked at the unhappy child, her brown curls framing her pixie face, and something stirred within her heart. It wasn't love that she felt, but it was a small step in the right direction. [25–31]

Love comes when we take the time to understand
and care for another person.

Whosoever shall give to drink unto one of these little ones a
cup of cold water . . . shall in no wise lose his reward.
MATTHEW 10:42

HELP

Remembering that Clark prayed before he ate, Marty bowed her head. Nothing happened. Then she heard the sound of pages being turned. She peeked at Clark and saw him, Bible in hand, turning the pages. "We read Psalm 121 today," he said. " 'I will lift up mine eyes unto the hills from whence cometh my help. The Lord is thy keeper: the Lord is thy shade upon thy right hand. The sun shall not smite thee by day, nor the moon by night. The Lord shall preserve thee from evil: he shall preserve thy soul. The Lord shall preserve thy going out and thy coming in from this time forth and even for evermore.' "

Gently Clark laid the book aside on a small shelf close to the table, and then bowed his head and prayed, "Our God, fer this fine day an' yer blessin's, we thank ya."

Blessin's, wondered Marty. *Like a howlin' kid, spilled coffee an' a burned finger. Blessin's?*

But Clark went on. "Thank ya, Lord, thet the first hard mile with Missie be traveled, an' help this one who has come to be her new mama."

He never calls me by my name when he's a talkin' to his God, thought Marty. *If his God is able to be answerin' his prayer, I hope He knows who he's talkin' 'bout. I need all the help thet I can git.* [32–33]

We can be grateful that God does indeed know us
all by name; we too need all the help we can get.
*I have called thee by thy name. . . . When thou passest through
the waters, I will be with thee.*
ISAIAH 43:2

MISTAKES

Marty awoke with a start, sensing that something was wrong. She sprang up, her heart pounding. Where was Missie? She looked inside and out, calling as she went. No Missie. She ranged farther and farther but still no Missie. She was getting frantic now in spite of her efforts to keep herself under control.

Tears streamed down Marty's cheeks. She checked the creek— up and down its banks, but no sign of Missie or of anything that belonged to her.

Marty set off down the dusty, rutted roadway. On and on she stumbled. Then she saw Clark's team coming toward her. When it stopped beside her she looked up at Clark, and there sat Missie as big as life on her pa's knee, looking very proud of herself.

The girl in Marty wanted desperately to cry, but the woman in her refused herself even that small comfort.   [38–39]

Mistakes sometimes turn into tragedy, but we can
be grateful that most of the time our pride is all
that gets hurt.

And when they found him not, they turned back. . . . After three
days they found him in the temple . . . about [his] Father's
business.
LUKE 2:45–49

NEEDS

Marty folded her worn dresses and undergarments. If only she had a needle and some thread. But she wouldn't ask him, she determined. Never!

As she sat down on her bed to find a more comfortable position for her self-pity, Marty noticed a small sewing basket in the corner behind the door. Crossing to the basket she discovered more than she had dared to hope for—thread of various colors, needles of several sizes, a perfect pair of scissors, and even some small pieces of cloth. Sewing was one thing Marty could do, though mending, she felt, hardly fit into the same category as sewing. Marty attacked the least worn items first, but by the time she reached the last few articles she was completely dejected. They'd never last the winter, but she would never ask him for anything. Even if she had nothing but rags.

Marty fell into bed and again cried herself to sleep. If only Clem were there, her world would be made right again. [41]

Sometimes we wish and pray for what we think
will make us happy, not realizing that we already
have it.

The eyes of your understanding being enlightened; that ye may know
. . . the riches of the glory of his inheritance.
EPHESIANS 1:18

APPRECIATION

Marty pulled the biscuits out of the oven and dumped one on the cupboard to cool. Then she slowly closed her teeth upon it—to no avail; the biscuit refused to give. She clamped down harder; still no give. "Dad-burn," she murmured, throwing the offensive thing into the stove. The flames around it hissed, like a cat with its back up, but the hard lump refused to disappear. "Dad-blame thing. Won't even burn." She crammed a stick of wood on top of it to cover up the telltale lump.

Marty looked around. How could she get rid of the lumpy things? She'd bury them. She scooped them into her skirt and out the door she went. At the far end of the garden, she fell on her knees, dug a hole with her hands, and dumped in the disgusting lumps. She covered them quickly and sprinted back to the house. When she reached the yard, she could smell burning ham.

"Oh, no!" she cried. "What a mess!"

For supper, Clark was served lukewarm mushy potatoes and slightly burned slices of ham along with the few slices of bread that remained. There was no mention of the carrots which had just begun to boil, and of course no mention of the sad lumps called biscuits. Clark said nothing as he ate. Nothing, that is, except, "That's right good coffee." [47–48]

Nothing is so bad that we can't say a kind word about it.
Everything God created is good and . . . is to be . . .
received with thanksgiving.
1 TIMOTHY 4:4

CARING

"How aire things goin', Marty?"

Marty's resolve to hold up bravely went crumbling. Words tumbled over words as she poured out all about endless pancakes, Missie's stubborn outburst, hard-as-rock biscuits, Missie's disappearance, the terrible supper she had served the night before, and, finally her deep longing for the man she had lost. Ma sat silently, her eyes filling with tears. Suddenly she rose.

"Come, my dear," she said gently. "You aire a-gonna have ya a lesson in bread makin'. Then I'll sit me down an' write ya out every recipe thet I can think of. It's a shame what ya've been goin' through the past few days, bein' as young as ya aire an' still sorrowin' an' all, an' if I don't miss my guess"—her eyes going over Marty—"ya be in the family way too, ain't ya, child?"

Marty nodded, and Ma took over, working and talking and finally making Marty feel worthwhile again. After a busy day Ma departed. She left behind her a reef of recipes with full instructions, fresh baked bread, a basket full of her own goodies and a much more self-confident Marty with supper well under control.

Marty breathed a short prayer that if there truly was a God, He'd see fit to send a special blessing upon this wonderful woman whom she had so quickly learned to love.   [54]

A caring heart and a simple deed can relieve
another's grief.
He careth for you.
1 PETER 5:7

SELFISHNESS

Marty realized that Clark was fighting for control. His lips trembled and she saw tears in his eyes. He had ordered the lovely new sewing machine for his Ellen's birthday, and now Ellen wasn't here to receive it. He must be suffering, too. Marty had never thought of him as hurting—of being capable of understanding how she felt. Hot tears washed down her cheeks. *Why do sech things, sech cruel things, happen to people? Why? Why?*

Marty knew there was no easy answer. This was the first time Clark had mentioned his wife. Marty had been so wrapped up in her own grief that she had not even wondered much about the woman who had been Clark's wife, Missie's mama, and the keeper of this house. Now her mind was awake to it. Everything in the house spoke of this woman. She had been so young, and she was already gone. Marty didn't even know how she died, but she now realized that there had been a woman in this house who made it a home, who gave birth to a baby daughter that she cherished, who shared days and nights with her husband. Then he had lost her and he hurt—hurt like she did over losing her Clem. She had been feeling that she was the only one in the world who bore that sorrow, but it wasn't so. [58–59]

Sometimes our own sorrow so consumes us that
we forget the needs of others.
*Look not every man on his own things, but . . . also on the things of
others.*
PHILIPPIANS 2:4

23

TIME

The stars blinked down at Marty from a clear sky.

"It's mean," she whispered, "but it's beautiful." What was it that Ma had said? "Time," she'd said; "it is time that is the healer—time an' God." Marty supposed that she meant Clark's God.

"Iffen we can carry on one day at a time, the day will come when it gets easier an' easier, an' one day we surprise ourselves by even bein' able to laugh an' love agin." That's what Ma had said.

It seemed so far away to Marty, but somehow she had the firm belief that Ma Graham should know. [59]

> When our days are filled with crying, we can trust
> that God, in time, will again bring laughter.
> *Blessed are ye that weep now: for ye shall laugh.*
> LUKE 6:21

MOTIVES

Marty's fingers fumbled as she lit the lamp. Then she hurried to try to untie the store string. She was unprepared for what she found when the brown paper fell away.

There was material there for undergarments and nighties and enough lengths for three dresses. She dug farther and found a pattern for a bonnet and two pieces of material.

There was lace for trimming, and long warm stockings, and even a pair of shoes, warm and high for the winter, and a shawl for the cool days and evenings, and on the bottom, of all things, a long coat. Her eyes shone and her hands trembled. Then with a shocked appeal to her senses, she pulled herself upright.

"Ya little fool," she muttered. "Ya can't be a-takin' all this. Iffen ya did, ya'd be beholden to thet man fer years to come."

Anger filled Marty. She wanted the lovely things, but she would not humble herself to be "beholden" to this man. She would not be a beggar in his home. But could it be that he was embarrassed by her shabbiness? Yes, she decided, it could well be. Again her chin came up. Okay, she'd take it—all of it. She would not be an embarrassment to any man.

But what she knew, or thought she knew, drained much of the pleasure from the prospect of the new clothes.   [60–61]

When we question a person's motives for doing good, we do that person and ourselves an injustice.

Judge not . . . but consider . . . the beam that is in thine own eye.
MATTHEW 7:1–3

APPROACHING

Sunday was a cool day with a wind blowing from the west. After the morning Bible reading and prayer Marty's mind stayed with the scripture. Clark was still reading from the Psalms, and Marty often found herself puzzled over some of the words. She was listening more closely now, and she often felt herself wanting to ask Clark to repeat slowly some portion so that she might ponder over its meaning.

Could Clark's God be a comfort to others as He had been to the writer David? Marty yearned to know more about Clark's God; Bible reading hadn't been a part of her upbringing. On occasion Clark would give a few words of his own as a background or setting to the scripture for that day, telling a bit about the author and his life at the time of his writing. Marty knew that the words were for her understanding, but she didn't resent it. Indeed, she drank it in as one thirsting for knowledge.

This morning, as Clark prayed, Marty wondered if she dared approach Clark's God in the direct way that Clark did. She longed to do so but she held back. [82]

Leading people to God by the way we live, rather
than pushing them to acknowledge Him, can
relieve their fear of approaching Him
for the first time.

Ye are our epistle written in our hearts, known and read of all me.
2 CORINTHIANS 3:2

LOOKING FORWARD

O h, my, Christmas be only two weeks away an' I haven't even been a-thinkin' on it," Marty realized. Her mind went plunging from thought to thought so that she missed the rest of Clark's prayer. "Ya know," she ventured a little later, "I had fergot all 'bout how close Christmas be."

"I know Christmas be a mite hard to be a-thinkin' on this year. Iffen it be too hard fer ya, we can most ferget the day, 'cept fer the reading of the Story an' maybe a sock fer young Missie."

Marty thought for a few minutes.

"No," she finally answered. "Thet wouldn't be right. Missie needs her Christmas—a proper one like, an' I reckon it may do us good, too. We can't stay back there in the past nursin' our sorrow—not fer her sake, nor fer our own. Christmas, seems to me, be a right good time to lay aside hurtin' an' look fer somethin' healin'."

Clark's eyes widened. He'd never heard a better sermon than the one he'd just heard from Marty. [107–108]

> Planning for the future is always better than
> lamenting the past.
> *For I know the thoughts that I think toward you . . .*
> *thoughts of peace and not of evil . . . to give you*
> *hope and a future.*
> JEREMIAH 29:11

27

This would be Marty's first Christmas away from home—the first Christmas for her to make for others rather than have others make for her. The thought made her feel both edgy and excited.

"Well," she started. "I'll git me to doin' some Christmas bakin'. Maybe Ma has some special recipes she'll share. Then we'll have a tree fer Missie. Christmas Eve we'll put it up after she be tucked in, an' we'll string popcorn, an' make colored chains, an' have a few candles fer the windows, an' we'll kill a couple of the finest roosters, an' I'll find me somethin' to be a-makin' fer Missie—"

"Roosters nuthin'." Clark said. "I'll go myself an' buy us a turkey from the Vickers. Missus Vickers raises some first-rate 'uns. Maybe there be somethin' we can be a-makin' fer Missie together. I'll ride over to Ma's today an' git the recipes, or better still, it looks like a decent day. Ya be wantin' me to hitch ole Dan an' Charlie so ya can be a goin' yerself?"

"Oh, could I?" Marty's voice was almost a plea. "I'd love to see Ma fer a chat iffen yer sure it be all right."

Marty's excitement was infectious. Clark, too, found himself caught up in the anticipation of the coming Christmas. [108–109]

Having something to look forward to can improve
our attitude and outlook, and Christians always
have something to look forward to.
Looking for . . . the glorious appearing of . . . Jesus Christ.
TITUS 2:13

Christmas Day! Marty opened her eyes earlier than usual and already her head was spinning. She had so much to do to get ready for the Grahams' arrival. She dressed quickly and hurried to the kitchen. She shivered as she moved to start the fire. Her hands already felt numb. She could hear the wind whining around the cabin as she coaxed the blaze to take hold. She moved into the sitting room to light the fire there. When both fires were burning she turned to the frost-covered window. Scratching a small opening with her fingers, she pressed her face to the pane to look out on Christmas Day. An angry wind swirled heavily falling snow, piling drifts in mountainous proportions.

Marty didn't need to be told that she was witnessing a dreaded prairie blizzard. The pain of it all began to seep in, taking possession of her. She wanted to scream out against it, to curse it away, to throw herself on her bed in a torrent of tears. She felt weary and defeated. She was licked. She felt dead again. Then suddenly a new anger took hold of her. Why should the storm win?

"Go ahead," she stormed at the raging wind. "Go ahead and howl. We have the turkey ready to go in the oven. We have lots of food. We have our tree. We have Missie—we'll still have Christmas even if the Grahams can't come!"   [114–115]

> We defeat only ourselves when we let
> circumstances determine our attitude.
> *And having food and raiment let us be therewith content.*
> 1 TIMOTHY 6:8

UNDERSTANDING

W e'll have to cook the whole turkey," Marty thought aloud, "but we can freeze what we can't eat. I'll put the vegetables in smaller pots an' cook only what we be a-needin'. The rest will keep fer a while in the cold pit. The bakin' "—she laughed as though it were a hopeless thing—"we be eatin' thet 'til spring iffen we don't get some help."

"Thet's one thing thet I don't be complainin' 'bout," Clark said. "Here I was a-worryin' 'bout all those Graham young 'uns with their hefty appetites a comin' an' not leavin' anythin' fer me, an' now look at me, blessed with it all."

"Clark," Marty said in mocked shock, "did you go an' pray this storm?" She'd never heard him laugh so heartily before. "Seems the storm nearly won," Marty acknowledged, "but it can't win unless ya let it, can it?"

Clark said nothing but his eyes told her that he understood her disappointment—and more than that, her triumph over it.

"I'm right proud of ya," he said, touching her hand.

He had never touched her before except for helping her in and out of the wagon. Something about it sent a warm feeling through her. Maybe it was just knowing that he understood.   [116]

Having someone who understands is a great
blessing for ourselves. Being someone who
understands is a great blessing to others.
*We have . . . an high priest . . . [that can] be touched with the feeling
of our infirmities.*
HEBREWS 4:15

PAIN & PLEASURE

Hearing the commotion, Clark emerged, pale-faced, from the lean-to. "Now ya stop a-frettin'," Ma said to him. "She be carryin' the baby well. It only be a matter of time 'til ya be a-holdin' 'im in thet rockin' chair."

At a cry from Marty, Ma hurried off and Clark sank, even whiter, into a chair. "Oh, God," he prayed, "it's up to you an' Ma now. Please help Ma." There was no Amen, for Clark didn't end his prayer. He continued it through the trying day.

Marty carried on, taking one pain at a time, her lips stifling the screams that wanted to come. Ma stayed close by, giving words of encouragement and administering what little comfort she could. At fifteen to four, Marty gave a sharp cry that ended as a baby boy made his appearance into the world. Marty lay exhausted, but a smile crossed her face as she heard her son cry.

Clark looked down on a worn-out Marty. Her damp, loose hair showed the signs of her tossing, but she smiled up gallantly. His gaze shifted to the small bundle. One small clenched fist lay against his cheek. "He's a real dandy," Clark said at last. Then he finished his prayer. "Thank ya, Father, fer helpin' Ma, and fer Marty's safe birthin' an' thet fine new boy." This time he said, "Amen." [131–133]

Intense pain often precedes immense pleasure.

I take pleasure in infirmities . . . when I am weak, then am I strong.

2 CORINTHIANS 12:10

LOVE

There's more than one way thet love comes," Ma explained to Marty. "Oh, sure, sometimes it comes wild-like, makin' creatures into wallerin' simpletons, but it doesn't have to be thet way, an' it's no less real an' meanin'ful iffen it comes another way. Ya see, Marty, sometimes love sorta steals up on ya gradual like, not shoutin' bold words or wavin' bright flags. Ya ain't even aware it's a-growin' an' gettin' stronger until all the sudden it takes ya by surprise like, an' ya think, 'How long I been a-feelin' like this an' why didn't I notice it afore?' "

Marty stirred. It was strange to get a look inside of Ma, to see her as a young girl, widowed like herself, with pain and heartaches, doing what she had felt was best for her children. She rose to get more coffee and turned her thoughts to the now. Ma was happy again, and she loved Ben. Just how or when it happened she couldn't really say, but it had. Love just worked its way into her heart—slowly, softly.   [136–137]

God's love doesn't always come waving flags,
either. It too can "steal up on ya gradual like."
God commendeth his love toward us . . . while we were

yet sinners.
ROMANS 5:8

BLAME

I'm sorry. I really am," Marty's neighbor stammered. "I didn't know I'd react so foolishly at seein' your new baby. I—I'd love to have a baby. My own, you know. Well, I have had babies of my own—three in fact, but they've not lived . . ." Her voice trailed off. Then anger filled her eyes. "It's this wretched country! If I'd stayed back East things would have been different. It's this horrible place. Look what it did to you. Losing your husband and having to marry a stranger to survive. It's hateful—just hateful!"

By now the young woman was sobbing. Marty crossed to Wanda, laying a sympathetic hand on her shoulder. "I'm so sorry," she said. "Why, iffen I'd lost young Clare, I don't know iffen I could of stood it. I jest can't know how ya must feel, a losin' three babies an' all, but I know ya must hurt awful."

Marty placed her arms around the shaking shoulders and pulled the young woman against her. "It's hard, it's truly hard to be a losin' somethin' thet ya want so much, but it could happen any-where. Womenfolk back East sometimes lose their young'uns too. Ya mustn't hate this land. Don't do a lick a good to be a fightin' the way things be, when there be nuthin' a body can do to change 'em." [140]

It's natural to want to blame something or someone
for bad circumstances, but doing so only gives us
a handle with which to hang on to bitterness.
Follow peace with all men . . . lest any root of bitterness
springing up trouble you.
HEBREWS 12:14, 15

FEELINGS

In the evenings Clark and Marty were happy to rest before the open fire, Marty with her quilt pieces or knitting, Clark with one of his books or some kind of light work.

As they worked, they talked, sharing events that made up their little world. The early fall and long winter had brought the animals down from the hills in search of food. Lately a couple of coyotes had been moving in closer at nights, causing poor Ole Bob a great deal of noisy concern.

The neighbors were rarely seen during the winter months, so news was scarce. Measles had been reported in the town, but no serious cases had been heard of. They talked of the spring planting and of the hope that spring would be early in coming. They shared the cute things that Missie said and the progress report of Clare.

Marty found it increasingly easy to talk to Clark. In fact, she looked forward to relating the events of the day. They discussed "little things" in their evenings, yet in doing so they were discovering deeper things about each other without realizing it. Feelings, dreams, hopes and faith were shared in a relaxed, simple way. [148–149]

Little feelings are important, because they grow to be big attitudes.

Thy servant slew both the lion and the bear: and this . . .
Philistine shall be as one of them.
1 SAMUEL 17:36

PRAYER FOR OTHERS

One evening as Marty quilted and Clark sanded the headboard for Missie's new bed, their talk turned to the scripture they had read at breakfast. A lot of the words were without meaning to Marty.

"Do ya really think thet God, who runs the whole world like, be a-knowin' you?" she asked.

"I'm right sure thet He do," Clark responded simply, " 'cause He answers so many of my prayers."

"Ya mean by givin' ya whatever ya ask fer?"

"No, not thet. Ofttimes He jest helps me to git by without what I asked fer. A lot of times, what folks ask fer they don't a'tall need. Like good crops, new plows, an extry cow or two."

"What about iffen ya lose something thet ya already had an' had sorta set yer mind on, like Clem or Ellen?"

"He don't take away the hurt, but He shares it with ya."

"Wisht I woulda had me someone to share mine with."

"He was there, an' I'm a-thinkin' thet He helped ya more than ya knowed."

"But I didn't really ask Him to."

"I did." [149–150]

When others don't know how to pray for
themselves, God answers our prayers on
their behalf.

Pray for one another.
JAMES 5:16

NECESSITIES

Marty had barely fallen asleep when she was awakened. Clark was bending over her, pulling on his jacket as he spoke. "The barn be ablaze. Ya jest stay put. I'm goin' fer the stock."

Marty jumped from her bed and ran to the kitchen window. "No, Clark, no. Don't go in there, please, please—" Marty's own voice choked her. She stood silently, praying as best she could. "Oh, God, iffen yer there, please let 'im come out." But the next dark figure to come through the smoke was a milk cow, then another, and another. "Oh, God!" sobbed Marty, "he'll never make it." The walls of the barn were engulfed in flame now. But then she saw him, stumbling through the entrance, staggering until he reached the corral fence where he leaned for support.

The long night blurred on. Neighbor men, with water and snow, fought to save the other buildings. Morning came. The barn lay in ruins, but the other buildings had been saved.

Clark pulled Marty gently into his arms. "Oh, Clark," she whispered, "what aire we gonna do now?"

Clark answered calmly. "Well, we aire gonna pray, an' what He sees us to be a-needin', He'll give; an' what He sees we don't need, He'll make us able to do without."   [153–155]

In his graciousness, God gives us many luxuries;
we make a mistake when we consider
them necessities.

*The fowls . . . do . . . not gather into barns; yet your heavenly
Father feedeth them.*
MATTHEW 6:26

FINDING GOD

Parson Simmons related the simple story of Easter, beginning with Christ's ministry to the people of His day, His arrest and the false accusations, and His sentence of death.

Marty had heard how men had put Christ to death with no just cause, but never before had she realized that it had anything to do with her. The fact that He personally took the punishment for her sins, as well as for the sins of all mankind, was a startling and sobering discovery.

"I didn't know thet ya died fer me," her heart cried. "I'm sorry—truly I am. Lord, I asks ya to be a-doin' what yer intendin' in my heart."

The preacher then told about the women who found that the Lord had risen. "He lives," said the preacher, "and because He is victor over sin and death, we too can be."

Marty's heart filled with such a surge of joy that she felt like shouting. She had to tell someone that now she understood. She had given herself to be a-knowin' Clark's God. She reached down and slipped her small hand into his strong one. Clark looked at her, reading the difference in her face, and the big hand firmly clasped the small one. Marty knew that he shared her joy, as she now shared his God. [166–167]

> Sharing God with others, unlike sharing anything
> else, does not diminish our portion.
> *Philip findeth Nathanael, and saith unto him, we have*
> *found . . . Jesus.*
> JOHN 1:45

UNIQUENESS

After the dinner dishes were done and the children were sleeping, Clark and Marty spread their garden seeds out on the kitchen table to decide what was to be put in at first planting and what left until later. Clark patiently showed her the different seeds, telling her what they were and the peculiarity of their growing habits. Marty listened wide-eyed. He knew so much, Clark did, and as he talked about the seeds, they took on personalities right before her eyes—like children, needing special care and attention. [172]

People, like children and seeds, have unique
characteristics that require special handling
and treatment.

O Lord thou has searched me, and known me. Thou knowest
my downsitting and mine uprising, thou understandest my
thought afar off. Thou compassest my path and my lying
down, and art acquainted with all my ways.
PSALM 139:1–3

SORROW

Laura's body was carried to the Grahams'. Marty was there when it arrived. She would never forget the heartrending scene that she witnessed. Ma gathered the lifeless body into her arms, sobbing as though her heart would break, saying over and over, "My poor baby, my poor little darlin'." Then, after letting her grief drain from her, she wiped her tears, squared her shoulders and tenderly began to prepare the body for burial. Ben's grief matched Ma's, but he being a man did not feel the freedom in expressing it. Marty had never seen such an ashen face. She feared even more for Ben than for Ma.

Neighbors came, and neighbors set to work. The coffin was built and the grave dug, and the frail body of the girl was committed to the ground. In the absence of a preacher, Clark was asked to say the "buryin' " words. Marty could sense just how difficult it was for him.

Solemnly they all turned from the new mound, leaving Ma and Ben to sort out and adjust to their grief. It would take time, but Ma had said that time was the answer.   [176–177]

When the question is sorrow, time will answer it.
Ye shall be sorrowful, but your sorrow shall be turned into joy.
JOHN 16:20

STRENGTH

Marty walked past the buildings and down to the stream. She seemed drawn to the quiet spot she had discovered long ago when she had needed comfort—then because of her own loss and now because of Ma's.

She needed a place to think, to sort things out. Life was so confusing—the good so mixed up with the bad; such a strange combination of happiness and sorrow. She leaned against a tree trunk, watching the clear gurgling water flow.

"God," she questioned, "what be it all 'bout? I don't understand much 'bout ya. I know thet yer good. I know thet ya loved me 'nough to die fer me; but I don't understand all 'bout losin' an' hurtin'. I don't understand at all."

She closed her eyes, letting the strength of the sturdy tree trunk uphold her, listening to the rustling of the leaves, feeling the slight breeze ruffling her hair.

There was a strength there in the woods. She closed her eyes more tightly, drawing from it. [179]

Strength comes in quietness.
In quietness and confidence shall be your strength. (NIV)
ISAIAH 30:15

When Marty opened her eyes, Clark was sitting against a tree. He picked up a small branch and broke off small pieces that he watched the stream carry away.

"Guess life be somethin' like thet stream," he said. "Leaves stomp it up—animals waller in it—spring floods fill it with mud." He hesitated. "Bright sunshine makes it like a mirror glass, sparklin' rain makes it grow, but it still moves on—unchangin' like—the same stream even with the changes. It breaks through the leaves, it clears itself of the animal wallerin'—the muddy waters turn clean agin. Life's like thet—bad things come but life keeps on a-flowin', clearin' its path gradual like, easin' its own burden. The good times come; we maybe could make do without 'em, but He knows thet we need 'em to give meanin'—to strengthen us, to help us reflect the sunshine. Guess one has to expect the good an' the bad, long as we be a-livin', an' try one's best to make the bad hurt as little as possible, an' the good—one has to help it grow like, make all the good count."

Clark was right. Life was like that stream. It went on. Marty was ready to go on now, too. She had drawn strength from the woods. No, that was wrong. She had drawn strength from the God who made the woods.   [179–180]

Seeing how God works in nature can help us
understand how He works in our lives.
*For the invisible things of him from the creation of the world
are clearly seen.*
ROMANS 1:20

LOVE'S ENDURING

PROMISE

ASSURANCE

Marty could feel it close in about her even as she thought about it. The broken wagon—the howling blizzard pulling and tearing at the flapping canvas, and she, Marty, huddled alone in a corner, vainly clasping a thin, torn blanket about her shivering body in an effort to keep warm. Her despair at being alone was more painful than the cold that sought to claim her.

"I'm gonna die," she thought, "all alone. I'm gonna die"—and then she awakened and felt the warmth of her own four-poster bed. She looked through the cabin window at a sky blessed with stars and could not suppress another shiver. As it passed through her body, a strong arm went about her, drawing her close.

She hadn't meant to waken Clark. His days had been such busy ones, and she knew that he needed his sleep. As she studied his face in the pale light from the window, she realized that he really wasn't awake—not yet.

A flood of love washed over her. Whenever she needed assurance of his love, it was given her, even from the world of sleep; for this was not the first time that he had sensed her need, even before he awakened, and drawn her close.   [9–10]

Mature love senses a loved one's need and reaches
out immediately to meet it.

That their hearts might be comforted, being knit together in
love, and unto all riches of the full assurance of understanding.
COLOSSIANS 2:2

T he fire was soon crackling. Marty put the kettle on to boil and then filled the coffeepot. It would be awhile before the stove warmed the kitchen and the coffee began to boil, so Marty pulled her robe about her for warmth and took Clark's worn Bible from the shelf. She'd have time to read and pray before the family began to stir.

She felt especially close to God this morning. The dream had made her aware again of how much she had to be thankful for, and the anticipation of the new school added to her feeling of well-being. Only God really understood her innermost self. She was glad for the opportunity to pour it all out to Him.

Marty sat slowly sipping the hot coffee, enjoying the luxury of the liquid spreading warmth to her whole being. She felt refreshed now, both physically and spiritually. Again her eyes sought out the verse that had seemed meant just for her at this particular time. "Be strong and of a good courage, be not afraid, neither be thou dismayed; for the Lord thy God is with thee whithersoever thou goest." [12]

A quiet morning with a loving God puts the events
of the upcoming day into proper perspective.

Be quiet: fear not.
ISAIAH 7:4

COMMUNICATION

Alone. The word was a haunting one. She was so thankful that she was not alone. Again in humbleness she acknowledged the wisdom of her Father in leading her so quickly to Clark after the death of Clem. She realized now that as soon as she had healed sufficiently to be able to reach out to another, Clark was already there, eager to welcome her. Why had she fought God's provision for her with every fiber of her being? Ma Graham had said that it took time for healing, and Marty was sure that that was the reason. Given that time, she had been able to love again.

To love and be loved—to belong, to be a part of another's life—what a precious part of the divine plan.

Had she ever been able to really tell Clark all that she felt? Somehow to try to put it into words seemed never to do it justice. Oh, she tried to express it verbally, but words were so inadequate. Instead she sought to say it with her eyes, her actions; indeed, her very being responded to him in a hundred ways.   [12–13]

God has given us two ways to
communicate—with words and with actions. We
need both to do the job right.

*And when he had thus spoken, he showed them his hands
and his feet. . . . And they worshipped him, and returned . . . with*

great joy.
LUKE 24:40, 52

TIME FOR LOVE

I'd better hurry," Clare said as he slid off the chair. "Pa needs me."

Marty smiled. *Sure,* she thought, *Pa needs ya—needs ya to git in his way when he's feedin'; needs ya to insist on draggin' along a pail thet's too big fer ya; needs ya to slow his steps when he takes the cows back to pasture; needs ya to chatter at him all the time he's a doin'.* She shook her head but the smile remained. Yah, he needs ya—needs yer love an' yer idolizin'.

She helped Clare into a warm coat, put his hands into his mittens and his cap on his head, and opened the door for him. He set out briskly to find his pa. [17]

Getting things accomplished isn't nearly as important as taking time for love.
By love serve one another.
GALATIANS 5:13

PRECIOUS HURT

Marty glanced out of the kitchen window and saw her men coming from the barn. Clark's normally long strides were restrained to accommodate the short, quick steps of little Clare. Clare hung on to the handle of a milk pail, deceiving himself into thinking that he was helping to carry the load, and chattered at Clark as he walked. Ole Bob bounded back and forth before them, assuming that he was leading the way and that without him the two would never reach their destination.

Marty swallowed a lump in her throat. Sometimes love hurt a little bit—but oh, such a precious hurt. [18]

Love that gives the greatest pleasure can cause the greatest pain.

God so loved . . . that he gave his . . . Son.
JOHN 3:16

WEARINESS IN WELL-DOING

B uilding the school was hard work, made lighter only by the number who shared it and the satisfaction that it would bring.

The early spring sun grew almost hot, and men discarded their jackets as the work made their bodies grow warm.

The old stove cheerily did its duty—coffee boiled and large kettles of stew and pork and beans began to bubble, spreading the fragrance throughout the one-day camp.

A child stopped in play to sniff hungrily, and a man, heaving a giant log, thought ahead to the pleasure of stopping for the midday meal. At the stove, a woman who stirred the pot imagined her child doing sums at a yet unseen blackboard.

The sun, the logs, the laughter—but most of all, the promise—made the day a good one. They would go home weary, yet refreshed—bodies aching but spirits uplifted. Together they would accomplish great things, not just for themselves, but for future generations. They had given of themselves, and many would reap the benefits.

Maybe Ben Graham said it best as they stood gazing at the new structure before they turned their teams toward home.

"Kinda makes ya feel tall like." [20]

Weariness caused by well-doing makes us feel
worthwhile.

*Laboring night and day . . . we preached unto you the gospel
of God. . . . For what . . . is our crown of rejoicing? . . . Even ye.*
1 THESSALONIANS 2:9, 19

He's here. It's another fine son."

"Missie will be disappointed," Marty almost whispered.

"No one could be disappointed for long over this boy," Doc said. "He's a dandy." In the light of the lamp, Marty could see that he was indeed a dandy; and love for the new life spread through her.

Clark beamed as he gazed at his new son. "Another prize-winner, ain't he now?" he said proudly. Then he left, soon to return with a sleepy-eyed child in each arm.

"Yer new brother," he said. "Look at 'im sleepin' there. Ain't he jest fine?"

"A boy?" Missie asked. "I prayed fer a girl."

"Sometimes, God knows better than us what is best. He knows thet what we want might not be right fer us now; so, sometimes, 'stead of givin' us what we asked Him fer, He sends what He knows to be best fer us. Guess this baby boy must be someone special fer God to send him instead."

Missie listened carefully; then a smile spread over her face as the baby stretched and yawned in his sleep.   [24–25]

When we pray for what we want we should keep
in mind that only God knows what we need.

If ye then, being evil, know how to give good gifts unto your
children, how much more shall your Father which is in heaven
give good things to them that ask him?
MATTHEW 7:11

THE BEST

Y a don't know Cameron Marshall too well yet, do ya?" Clark asked. "He's a rather strange man. It's jest like Cam to feel thet his boy's gotta be the smartest, his girl the prettiest. I think thet be the reason why he married Wanda. He figured thet she was the prettiest girl so she had to be his. His problem is his emphasis on 'mine's the best.' One time Cam saw a fine horse. He jest had to have it 'cause it was a little better'n eny other horse in these parts. Sold all his seed grain to git thet horse. Set 'im back fer years, but guess he figured it was worth it.

"Ever notice his wagon? All painted up an' with extry metal trimmin's. Could have had a bigger place to live. A few years back men of the neighborhood helped him log so's he could build. 'Stead, he saw thet wagon, so he sold the logs an' bought it—an' he an' Wanda still live in thet one little room. The way Cam sees it, a house belongs to the woman, not the man. Often wished thet he'd take him a notion thet he had to have the best house, too; might find 'im a way to git one. Sure would be easier fer Wanda—an' now with a baby comin', they sure do need more room.

"Often wondered what would make a man feel thet he had to prove hisself by gittin' things. Somethin' deep down must be troublin' Cam to have made 'im like he is." [28–29]

Having nice things doesn't make a person nice.

Covet earnestly the best gifts.
1 CORINTHIANS 12:31

ASKING WHY

I'm so sorry thet ya be down," Marty said to Mrs. Larson. "I didn't hear of it 'til today. Jedd should have called and let us know an' we could of been over to help sooner.

"Nice thet ya got those two fine girls to be a helpin'. When I came, Nandry was washin' up the dishes an' Clae a-sweepin' the floor. Must be a great comfort to ya—them girls."

Mrs. Larson's eyes looked more alive. She nodded slightly. Marty knew how she loved her girls.

"Must be a real tryin' time fer ya. A woman jest hates to git down—hates to not be a-carin' fer her family. Makes one feel awful useless like, but God, He knows all 'bout how ya feel—why yer sick. There's always a reason fer His 'llowin', though we can't always see it right off like. I'm sure thet there be a good reason fer this, too. Someday, maybe we'll know why." [32–33]

God doesn't mind us asking "why," but we don't
always understand His answer right away.
*My God, my God, why hast thou forsaken me? . . . He is not
here: for he is risen.*
MATTHEW 27:46; 28:6

Could God show love to young'uns of a sinful woman?" Mrs. Larson pleaded.

"Yes," Marty said. "He loves the girls, an' I'm sure He will help 'em. But, Mrs. Larson, He loves you, too, an' He wants to help you. I know thet ya be a sinner, but we all be no different. The Book says thet we all be a-sinnin' an' a-hangin' on to our sin like it be somethin' worthwhile keepin', but it's not. We gotta let go of it, and God will take it from us an' put it there in thet big pile of sin thet Jesus took on hisself thet day He died. It isn't our goodness thet makes us fittin' to share heaven with Him. It's our faith. We jest say 'thank ya, Lord, fer dyin', an' clean me up on the inside so's I'll be fittin' fer yer heaven'—an' He will. All in answer to our prayer of askin'. Do ya want to pray, Mrs. Larson? Jest tell Him thet yer done hangin' on to yer sins—thet ya don't want to carry 'em enymore, an' would He please git rid of 'em fer ya. Then thank Him too—fer His love an' His cleanin'."

Mrs. Larson began her short prayer. The faltering words gradually gathered strength and assurance. When Marty opened her eyes, she saw a weak, yet confident, smile.

"He did!" Mrs. Larson exclaimed. "He did!" [33–34]

God doesn't pry us away from our sins. He insists that we
let go of them ourselves before He carts them away.
*If we confess our sins, he is faithful and just to forgive us our
sins, and to cleanse us from all unrighteousness.*
1 JOHN 1:9

PATIENCE

The children now spent time outside in the sunshine. Clare went with Clark whenever possible, and Missie enjoyed bundling up little Arnie and taking him out to play. When she tired of caring for the baby, she would bring him back indoors and return outside to dig around in a bit of ground that she dubbed "my garden." Marty had given her a few seeds, and already a few shoots of green showed where a turnip or some lettuce was making an appearance. Missie found it difficult to leave them alone and often was admonished for digging them up to see how they were doing. Her "garden" would have been much further along but for its periodic set-backs.

Marty was about ready to ask Clark if he would turn the soil in the big garden but cautioned herself not to get into too big a rush. The nights were still cool, and early plants may yet be damaged by frost. Still, it was hard to wait. [39]

Maturity teaches us the necessity of patience, but
it's still difficult to achieve.

Follow after . . . patience.
1 TIMOTHY 6:11

A PAINFUL GIFT

Word came to Clark and Marty on a rainy Wednesday afternoon that Mrs. Larson had quietly slipped away in her sleep. The funeral was planned for the next day. At two in the afternoon the wagons slowly made their way to a sheltered corner of Jedd's land where a short service was performed.

Marty's heart ached for the two girls standing huddled together in the rain as they watched their only source of love and comfort lowered into the ground. She dared to go to Jedd after the service and suggest that she would be glad to take the girls home with her for a few days until things were "sorted out."

"Be no need," he answered. "There be plenty to home to keep their minds an' hands busy."

Marty felt anger rise sharply within her and turned away quickly to keep from expressing it. She wouldn't forget her promise to Tina Larson to help her daughters get an education. She would fight as long as she could to fulfill it—yet how was it ever to be accomplished? She'd pray harder. God had mysterious ways of answering prayer, beyond man's imagination. She bit her lip to stop its quivering, wiped the tears that were mingling with the rain on her cheeks, and went to join Clark, who was waiting in the wagon. [45–46]

The ability to share a person's grief is a gift from
God, but a painful one to accept.
Weep with them that weep.
ROMANS 12:15

STUBBORNNESS

Ma, I really came to talk 'bout Nandry and Clae. Ya know thet I promised Tina Larson thet I'd do all I could to see thet her girls had a chance fer their schoolin', an' Jedd—well, I jest fear thet he won't be 'llowin' no sech thing. In jest a few months now thet schoolhouse will be openin' its door, an' Jedd Larson declares thet no daughter of his be a needin' it."

Marty looked at Ma, the helplessness showing in her eyes.

"What we gonna do to make 'im change his mind?"

"Reckon there ain't much of enythin' thet will make Jedd Larson change his mind, lessen he wants to. Me, I wouldn't even be knowin' where to begin to work on thet man. He ain't got 'im much of a mind, but what he has got sure can stay put."

"Yeah," Marty sighed and played with her coffee cup. There didn't seem to be much hope for her to keep her promise. What could she do? She had prayed and prayed, but Jedd did not seem to be softening in the slightest toward the idea of schooling for his girls. Well, she'd just have to pray some more. Maybe somehow the Lord could open the mind of that stubborn man. [50]

Stubbornness and selfishness go hand in hand.
People who have one almost always have
the other.

Stubbornness is as iniquity and idolatry.
1 SAMUEL 15:23

ANSWERED PRAYER

T he school term was only a few weeks away, and there had been no change in Jedd Larson's attitude. Marty was about to concede that her prayers had been in vain. She was mulling over these thoughts as Clark read the morning scripture, "Ask an' it shall be given you; seek—"

I been askin', Lord, an' nothin's been happenin', she admonished her Lord and immediately felt remorse. *I'm sorry, Father*, she added. *I guess I'm 'bout the most faithless an' impatient child thet ya got. Help me to be content-like an' to keep on havin' faith.*

Sensing her mood, Clark prayed, "An', Lord, ya know thet school will be a-startin' soon an' ya know how Marty promised Mrs. Larson to try an' see thet the girls got their schoolin'. Only you can work in Jedd's heart to let her keep thet promise, Lord. We leave it to you to work out in yer own good way and time."

Maybe God would act now that Clark had prayed about it. Marty immediately reprimanded herself for her thought. She was God's child, too; and the Bible said that God did not regard one of His children above the other.

Later in the day Ole Bob announced an approaching team. It was Jedd Larson. Marty sensed an answer to prayer. [54]

Whether or not God will answer our prayers is not
a matter of question, but HOW He will answer
may leave us wondering.
*The eyes of the Lord are over the righteous, and his ears are
open unto their prayers.*
1 PETER 3:12

Did he agree?"

"Yeah, he agreed."

"Oh, Clark, thank ya. I never thought thet I'd be able to have the girls right here. He said thet we could keep them?"

"Well, he didn't exactly say fer how long, but I'll be surprised iffen Jedd Larson ever wants his girls back."

"Ya didn't make 'im pay their keep, did ya?"

"Well—not exactly," he said slowly. "Jedd said thet we could keep the girls iffen we gave 'im ten dollars a piece fer 'em."

Marty snorted. "I never thought thet I'd live to see the day thet one had to pay fer the privilege of feedin' another man's young'uns."

"Now, now," he said, "ya wanted yer prayers answered, didn't ya? Who are we to quibble as to how it be done? You've got a big job, Marty. Already ya have yer hands full with yer own young'uns. Addin' two more ain't gonna lessen yer load none. I hope yer tender heart don't jest break yer back."

"He answered our prayer, Clark. Iffen He thinks what we're doin' be right, then He'll give the strength thet we need too, won't He?"

Clark nodded. "I reckon He will." [58–59]

> Doing right is one decision we can make without
> considering the consequences.
> *As for the pure, his work is right.*
> PROVERBS 21:8

GOOD FORTUNE

True to his promise, Jedd arrived the next day with the two girls. Their few belongings were carried in a box and deposited in the bedroom that would be theirs. Marty wondered if the parting would be difficult for them, but there seemed to be no emotion shown by either side.

Jedd was anxious to be off. He had packed his possessions in his wagon, and with the money from the sale of the farm lying heavy in his pocket, he was hard-put to hold back, even for a cup of coffee. He did fill up on fresh bread and jam, however; and with the food barely swallowed, he announced that he must be on his way. He gave Marty and his two daughters a quick nod, which Marty supposed was to suffice for thank you, good-bye, and God bless you, and went out the door. He was full of the coming trip west and of all of the good fortune that he was sure it would hold. Jedd always had regarded good fortune more highly than hard work. [60]

Good fortune may bring quick reward, but only
hard work brings reliable income.
*And work with your own hands . . . that ye may have lack of
nothing.*
1 THESSALONIANS 4:11–12

COPY CAT

The town was filled with commotion. A wagon train was getting ready to move on. Dogs barked, horses stomped, and children ran yelling through the street. Grown men argued prices and women scurried about, running to the store for a last-minute purchase or looking for children who had been told to stay put but didn't. Marty decided that she had picked a poor day to come to town; surely her shopping would be slowed down considerably.

She entered the General Store with some trepidation. She always dreaded facing Mrs. McDonald's scrutinizing eyes and equally sharp tongue.

"I declare," she said to Clark on one occasion, "thet there woman's tongue has no sense of propriety."

Missie overheard the word and loved it. Henceforth she declared of all things—particularly to young Clare—"You've no sense of pa'piety," which seemed to be meaning "Yer jest plain dumb."

Marty guarded her tongue more carefully in Missie's presence after that. [66]

We never know who's listening to what we say . . .
or who's copying it.
Be ye followers of me, even as I also am of Christ.
1 CORINTHIANS 11:1

DISAPPOINTMENT

The boys returned from accompanying the girls to school. Marty changed them into dry clothes and made suggestions as to what they might like to do. She had thought herself prepared to deal with their disappointment but found that it was even worse than she had imagined.

Arnie fussed and refused to be pacified with toys. Clare insisted that he should be able to go to school, too. When he failed to convince Marty, he plagued her to let him go out to play. She pointed out the window at the rain, but Clare only whined and seemed to imply that Marty could do something about the weather if she would just put her mind to it.

Marty gave them each a cookie. Arnie shared his with Miss Puss and immediately undid all of his kindness by deliberately pulling the kitten's tail. She responded by scratching his hand. Arnie's howl brought Clare on the run. He chased the cat behind the kitchen stove and proceeded to poke at her with the broom handle. Marty despaired. What would she ever do with them through this long, long day?

[82–83]

Disappointment in adults as well as in children
can lead to bad behavior.

*And the soul of the people was much discouraged. . . . And the
people spake against God.*

NUMBERS 21:4–5

Guess what?" Missie said in a whisper. "Nathan LaHaye likes Clae. He pulled her braids an' everythin'."

Marty had no idea what the everythin' might be.

Then Missie's eyes took on fire. "But I hate thet Willie LaHaye. He's a show-off."

"Missie—shame on ya," admonished Marty. "We are not to hate anyone."

"Bet God didn't know 'bout Willie LaHaye when He made thet rule," Missie declared. "Nobody could love him. He reads real loud. And he reads everythin'—even the eighth primer. An' he teases too. He said thet I'm too cute to be dumb. He said he'd help me. I said, 'No, you won't,' an' he jest laughed an' said, 'Wait an' see.' Boy, he thinks he's smart."

Missie tossed her head, and Marty wondered where her little girl had gone so suddenly to be replaced by this arrogant creature who deemed herself a young lady.

Please, thought Marty, *don't let school change her thet much—thet fast*, but the next moment the little girl was back again. [83–84]

Growing spiritually is like growing physically.
Just when we think we've reached a new level of
maturity, we revert to our old, immature behavior.
Thou art the Christ. . . . I do not know the man.
MATTHEW 16:16; 26:72

GOOD EXAMPLES

The fall work had been completed, and the farmers' attention could now be turned to other things. A meeting of the community adults was called for on a Saturday afternoon in early October. All residents were invited to attend and very few refused the invitation.

Zeke LaHaye had sent word that though he felt that the meeting was a worthwhile one, he was hard put to keep up with his farm work and just couldn't spare the time.

The neighbors had already discovered that Zeke LaHaye could spare no time from his farming duties—not to honor the Lord's Day, not to help a neighbor, not for any reasons. Clark, who rarely made comment on a neighbor's conduct, confided to Marty: "Thet poor farm sure must be confused-like—first owner contents hisself to let everythin' stay at rest; next owner nigh drives everythin' to death. Makes me stop short-like an' look within. I hope thet I never git so land hungry and money crazy thet I have no time fer God, family, or friends." [100]

Plenty of people are examples of how not to live;
few illustrate how we should live.

Be thou an example of the believers.
1 TIMOTHY 4:12

THY WILL BE DONE

Oh, dear God," Ma prayed, "what ever are we gonna do?"

"Well, seems to me," Marty said, weighing every word, "ya have only a couple of choices. Ya can fight it an' lose your son, or ya can okay it and welcome an Indian daughter-in-law."

"Oh, dear God!" said Ma, her face going even whiter. She paced the floor between the table and the stove. Marty waited. Suddenly Ma's face began to restore its color.

"Marty," she said, "I jest thought me of a third choice. I won't fight it an' I won't encourage it, but I sure am goin' to do some prayin'."

"Prayin', how?"

"Prayin'—how do ya think?" The words fairly snapped from Ma. "It jest won't work, Marty. Never. An' I won't have my Tom hurt—shunned an' ridiculed. Grandchildren thet ain't grandchildren 'cause they're neither white nor brown. It ain't to happen, Marty."

"Iffen ya pray like thet, Ma," Marty spoke quietly, slowly, "will ya be askin' fer help or jest givin' orders?"

Ma stiffened. Tears slid down her cheeks. She knew Marty was right. [106–107]

How we pray reveals what we believe.
If we ask any thing according to his will, he heareth us.
1 JOHN 5:14

LOOK FOR THE GOOD

When Clark went to town the following Saturday, he returned with the sobering news that Mrs. McDonald was gravely ill. The Doc, who had been faithfully attending her, reported her problem as a severe stroke. One side was paralyzed, her speech was gone, and she was confined to her bed in serious condition. No hope for her complete recovery was given.

Mrs. Nettles and Widow Gray, from town, took turns with Mr. McDonald in round-the-clock nursing. The store had been put up for sale.

Marty felt sick at heart upon hearing the news. She had never liked Mrs. McDonald, and the news of her illness filled her with guilt feelings.

"Maybe iffen I'd really tried," she told herself, "maybe I could have found a lovable woman behind the pryin' eyes and probin' tongue."

But there was little relief to her in the "maybes."

"God," she prayed, "please forgive me. I've been wrong. Help me in the future to see good in all people. To mine it out like, iffen it seems buried deep."   [124]

> We should try to find the good in people before
> we read it in their obituaries.
>
> *Whatsoever things . . . are good . . . think on these things.*
> PHILIPPIANS 4:8

WORDS AREN'T ENOUGH

The sermon left Marty puzzled. The Reverend had a voice that was easy enough to listen to, though he did at times get a mite loud. It was the words that Marty had a problem with. There were so many of them that she didn't understand. She chided herself for her ignorance. As the people filed out Marty heard several comments of "Good sermon, Parson," and was more convinced than ever that she was terribly dull.

On the way home she asked, "Clark—what was he talkin' 'bout?"

Clark howled. "Be hanged iffen I know," he finally managed. "Don't s'pose there be a soul there who did."

"Thought it was jest me thet's dumb," admitted Marty, and Clark laughed again.

"Well," he said, getting himself under control, "I think the good parson was sayin' somethin' about man bein' a special creature, designed fer a special purpose, but I never did get rightly sorted out what thet purpose was."

"Maybe next Sunday he'll explain," Marty said.   [130–131]

To communicate the Good News, we need to know
more than the "right words"; we need to know
the listener.

*I count all things but loss for the excellency of the knowledge
of Christ Jesus.*
PHILIPPIANS 3:8

EDUCATION

After five sermons Marty gave up hope that the Reverend would ever explain his meaning. Others seemed to have given up also, for a few of the less ardent families had ceased to attend. The worship service wasn't as worshipful as many wished it to be.

Marty wished that the Reverend weren't quite so "edjecated." Her soul longed to be fed, and Sunday by Sunday she went home feeling empty. The words were pretty words, fancy words, and she was sure, very intellectual—but they were empty to one who could not understand.

They accepted their new minister—accepted him for who he was, for Whom he represented, for what he had come to do. They accepted him, but deep down inside, there was probably no one who cared much for him, though not one of them would have been disloyal enough to say so. [134–135]

An education doesn't help us serve God's cause if
it isolates us from those who need Him.
Where is the wise? . . . God made foolish the wisdom of this
world.
1 CORINTHIANS 1:20

FRIENDSHIP

I had to see you, Marty," Wanda said. "I know that the neighbors are all talking about Rett being different. And I know they think Cam and I aren't aware. But we know, Marty. I guess I've known from the time Rett was a small baby. I hoped and prayed that I'd be wrong—but I knew. For a while I wondered about Cam. And then—one night—he just spilled it all out—he'd known, too." Wanda stopped and her lips trembled for a moment. Then she went on. "Marty, have you ever seen a grown man cry? Really cry? It's awful—just awful. I just had to tell someone—someone who would understand. It was hard at first—really hard. But Marty, I want you to know that I wouldn't change it, not really. He has brought us so much joy." She looked at Marty, the tears glistening in her eyes. "You see, I asked God so many times for a baby. And He's given me one—a boy that will, in some respects, never grow up. I don't suppose that Rett will ever leave me, not even for school. I have my baby—for always."

"Oh, Wanda." Marty put her arms around her friend and they wept together. When their tears had washed away their sorrow and cleansed away the frustration, they were able to look together to the future with new acceptance and anticipation.   [137–138]

Truth and tears can clear the way to a deep and
lasting friendship.
So Jonathan grieved for David.
1 SAMUEL 20:34

OBSTACLES

Saw Cam today," Clark said. "He had Rett with 'im. Do ya know thet thet boy can already handle a team. Should've see'd Cam. Proud as punch. Says Rett's gonna be the best horseman in these here parts. Might too. Seems to be a natural with animals. Cam says he wouldn't be none surprised to see thet lad take 'im on the tamin' of a bear. Never says a word, but he seems to make the animals understand 'im. Mr. Cassidy says thet Cam never comes to town but he brings Rett either on the wagon beside 'im or up in front of 'im in the saddle."

Clark seemed to be deep in thought for a moment.

"Funny thing. Cam's changed. Watchin' 'im move about town with his son I noticed a thoughtfulness 'bout 'im. He ain't thinkin' on Cam Marshall no more. I think others note it, too. Seem to have new respect fer 'im someway. Thought as I watched 'im leavin' town with thet boy up there beside 'im handlin' the reins, 'There goes a real man.' "

[146]

The way we choose to go around an obstacle will determine whether we move toward God or away from Him.

Ye did run well; who did hinder you that ye should not obey the truth?

GALATIANS 5:7

UNEXPECTED LOSS

The community folk were pleased to learn that Tessie was going to make her schoolteacher husband, Mr. Whittle, a father. Mr. Whittle was well pleased with himself. To have a young and attractive wife who idolized him was a wonder in itself, and to be about to become a father put him on cloud nine.

The great day came and the doctor was sent for, but he left the next morning with tired eyes and a heavy heart. Both Tessie and her baby boy died during the night. The news shook the whole community. Mr. Whittle moved as one in a daze; the loss was beyond his comprehension.

The day of the funeral was cold and dreary. The pine box was lowered, the earth heaped upon it. Marty gazed at the fresh grave that held a young mother with a baby boy in her arms. "Oh, Tessie, who would have thought that you would be the first to be buried in this cemetery! Life be full of the unexpected."

Mr. Whittle never resumed classes. Toward the end of May, when the roses were beginning to bloom and the birds were building their nests, Mr. Whittle placed a bouquet of wild flowers on the mound of earth and returned to the East.   [161–162]

When the unexpected catches us off guard, the
Guard of the universe will catch us.
The LORD upholdeth all that fall, and raiseth up all those that
be bowed down.
PSALM 145:14

WORDS & DEEDS

Pastor Joseph Berwick arrived the same day that Clae Larson began her first classes in the country school. He boarded with the Watleys and when Mrs. Watley beheld the tall good-looking young man, she turned to her two daughters with a twinkle in her eyes. She gave the girls a sly wink and nodded the parson into the parlor where tea was served. But Parson Berwick was not content to sit and sip tea. Before the dust of his last trail had a chance to settle, he was off again to meet the inhabitants of the area whom he saw as potential members of his flock.

He was not above lending a helping hand either and spent some time cutting wood for the Widow Rider, helping pound a fencepost that Jason Stern was placing, and forking hay along with the Graham boys.

[166]

Wise words combined with good deeds is the most
effective way to tell others why we love God.
*And whatsoever ye do in word or deed, do all in the name of
the Lord Jesus.*
COLOSSIANS 3:17

REASONS

Clae looked up from her gardening at the approaching stranger. The new parson dismounted and presented himself in a courteous manner.

"I'm Parson Berwick," he said politely. "Is the teacher home?"

"I," she emphasized the word, "am the teacher."

He reddened. "Oh, then I guess I want to see you. Let's start over, shall we?" He stepped back, then forward again with an impish smile. "Hello there," he said, "I'm Pastor Berwick, new to your area, and I'm calling on each of my parishioners." He reached for her grubby hand and shook it firmly.

"I'm sorry," she stammered, looking at her dirt-covered hands.

"You've got dirt on your nose, too," he said with a smile. Clae rubbed the spot but only made it worse. He laughed, then wiped the smudge from her face with a clean handkerchief. "As I said, I'm calling on my parishioners. Can I expect to see you in church on Sunday?"

"Oh, yes," whispered Clae, and blushed at her foolishness.

With a twinkle in his eye, he mounted his horse and rode away.

So it was that Clae had trouble focusing her attention on the sermon, but she never missed a Sunday. [167–169]

God can use our actions for good even when our reasons aren't all they should be.

Whether in pretence, or in truth, Christ is preached.
PHILIPPIANS 1:18

KNOWLEDGE

Parson Joe was quick in establishing his place in the community. His willingness to lend a hand endeared him to the farmers.

"Not afraid to dirty his hands, thet one."

"No—nor to bend his back."

But the real reason for their nod of approval was the Sunday services. His prayers were not just wordy but full of sincerity, and his sermons were the highlight of the whole service. Simple, straightforward messages, brought right from the Bible, gave the people the nourishment they craved.

The congregation grew numerically and spiritually. Willie LaHaye never missed a Sunday, and even Zeke LaHaye put aside an occasional Sunday morning for worship. Some felt that the loss of his daughter Tessie had softened the man somewhat.

Claude Graham remarked to his twin brother, Lem, "The reason thet he fits here so well is thet he don't know nothin' from them books neither."

Lem replied, "Don't let him fool ya. He's got a lot more of a load there then he's throwin' out each Sunday. No use forkin' a whole haystack to growin' calves."

[170–171]

A wise person can assess spiritual maturity and
determine how much truth another can swallow.

The tongue of the wise useth knowledge aright.

PROVERBS 15:2

VALUES

Rett Marshall was handling a team of horses almost as good as a grown man. He loved creatures, tame or wild, and even had a young jackrabbit for a pet. A strange boy, people were saying, but now there was admiration in their voices.

Marty remembered a conversation she had overheard long ago.

"I often wonder how a man feels when he sees what his skill has done," Mrs. Vickers had said to the doctor. "Do ya ever wish thet maybe ya hadn't—well—hadn't fought quite so hard-like?"

"Of course not," the doctor answered. "I didn't make that life—the Creator did—and when He made it, I expect that He had good reason for doing as He did—and what that reason is, is His business."

Marty thought of this each time that she watched the boy whistle a bird down or make friends with a prairie dog. She thought of it, too, when she saw the love in Wanda's eyes or heard Cam's proud boasting. [175]

Our ideas of perfection reveal our real values.

Every man that striveth for the mastery is temperate in all things. Now they do it to obtain a corruptible crown; but we an incorruptible.

1 CORINTHIANS 9:25

POSSESSIONS

Marty felt a sickness go all through her. Willie was heading farther west. Willie was also planning to marry her Missie. She slipped quietly out to the kitchen, walked into the coolness of the pantry, and leaned her head against a cupboard door.

"Oh, dear God," she prayed, "please help 'im git this silly notion out of his head."

For the first time in her life Marty could feel some of what her mother must have felt, and understood why she had resorted to protests and pleadings.

Marty wrapped a warm shawl about her shoulders and stepped out into the crisp night air. She turned her face heavenward. "God," she said, "she's yer child. We have long since given her back to you. Ya know how I feel 'bout her leavin', but iffen it's in yer plan, help me, Father—help me to accept it an' to let her go. Lead her, God, an' take care of her—take care of my little girl." [193–194]

When everything we have belongs to God
we don't have to fret about who's caring for it.
*I . . . know my sheep . . . and . . . neither shall any man pluck them
out of my hand.*
JOHN 10:14, 28

TENDER TEARS

On the tenth of May, Willie left to seek his new land.

Missie had bidden him farewell in private.

Zeke LaHaye accompanied his son into town and puttered around at last-minute fixings and unnecessary purchases. When the time finally came for the group to be off, Zeke stepped forward and gave his son a hearty handshake and some last-minute cautionary advice, as he knew the boy's mother would have done had she been there.

"Be careful now, son. Be courteous to those ya meet, but don't allow yerself to be stepped on. Take care of yerself an' yer equipment. It'll only be of use to you iffen ya look after it. Keep away from the seamy side of things—I ain't needin' to spell thet out none. Take care, ya hear?"

Willie nodded, thanked his pa, and was about to turn to go when Zeke LaHaye suddenly cast aside all reserve and stepped forward to engulf his boy in a warm embrace. Willie returned the hug, acknowledging how good it felt to be locked in the arms of his father. The last thing Willie remembered seeing as he turned to go was Zeke LaHaye, big and weathered, brushing a tear from his sun-tanned face. [196–197]

No one ever gets so big, or so tough, that he has no need to cry.

I have heard thy prayer, I have seen thy tears.
2 KINGS 20:5

NURTURING

Marty's throat caught in a heavy lump. Willie had returned safely and this was his and Missie's wedding day.

"Ma," said Missie. "I've never said it before, but I want to thank you—thank you for coming into our lives, for making us so happy—me and Pa."

Marty held her breath. If she tried to speak she'd cry, so she only pulled her little girl closer and kissed the brown curly head.

Clark came in then and put his arms around both of them. His throat was tight as he spoke. "God bless ya both," he said, and kissed each of them. Then he placed his hand gently on Missie, tried to clear the hoarseness from his throat, and prayed in a low voice, "The Lord bless ya an' keep ya; the Lord make His face to shine upon ya, and be gracious unto ya; the Lord lift up His countenance upon ya and give ya peace—now an' always, Missie. Amen."

Missie blinked away tears and moved out into the hall. Clark reached for Marty. "It hurts a mite, doesn't it?" he whispered.

Marty nodded. "Oh, Clark—I love her so."

"I know ya do." He pulled her close and his hand stroked her shoulder. "Thet's why yer lettin' her go." [205–206]

All the nurturing we do for children and for each other
is for one purpose—so they'll no longer need us.

*We exhorted . . . you as a father doth his children, that ye would
walk worthy of God.*
1 THESSALONIANS 2:11–12

LOVE'S LONG

JOURNEY

When Missie opened her eyes she was surprised at the changes that had taken place around her. It was much cooler, and the sharp, pleasant smell of woodsmoke was heavy in the air. The odors of cooking food and boiling coffee made her insides twinge with hunger. Now fully awake, she looked around in embarrassment at the supper preparations. Willie would soon be back from caring for the animals—and not even find a fire started! Missie hurried toward her wagons. It took a moment for her to realize that the fire burning directly in front of their wagons was *her* fire, and that the delicious smell of stew and coffee came from *her* own cooking pots.

Willie looked relieved when he saw her. "Yer lookin' better. How ya feelin'?" he asked.

"I'm fine—just fine, but shamed nigh to death for sittin' there a-sleepin' in the middle of the day, an' you—you makin' the fire, an' the coffee an'—my goodness—what must they all think of me—that my husband has to do his work an' mine too?"

"Iffen thet's all thet's troublin' ya," Willie responded, "I reckon we can learn to live with it." [19–20]

Judging ourselves by what others think of us is
foolish because others know little or nothing about
us or our circumstances.

*Paul thought not good to take him with them . . . so Barnabas
took Mark.*
ACTS 15:38–39

GROWING UP

As Missie lifted the bread and the butter tarts from the crock, she envisioned Marty's flushed face as she bent over her oven, removing the special baking for the young couple she loved so dearly.

Willie seemed to sense Missie's mood; his arms went round her and he pulled her close.

"She'll be missin' you, too, long 'bout now," he said softly against her hair.

"I reckon she will," Missie whispered.

"Missie?" Willie hesitated. "Are ya sure? It's still not too late to turn back, ya know. Iffen yer in doubt. . . ? Iffen ya feel—?"

"My goodness, no!" Missie said emphatically. "There's not a doubt in my mind at all. I'm lookin' forward to seein' yer land and buildin' a home. You know that! Sure, I'll miss Mama an' Pa an' the family—'specially at first. But I just gotta grow up, that's all. Everyone's gotta grow up *sometime*." How could Willie think that she was so selfish as to deny him his dream?   [20–21]

Growing up doesn't always mean leaving loved
ones behind, but it does require leaving some
loved things behind. As we take on responsibility,
we must give up some of our freedom.
But grow up unto him in all things. . . . Don't give place to the
devil.
EPHESIANS 4:15–27

NOURISHED BY THE WORD

After they had finished their meal together and Missie had washed the few dishes, Willie brought out their Bible. It was carefully wrapped in oiled paper with an inner wrap of soft doe-skin.

"Been thinkin'," he said. "Our mornin's are goin' to be short and rushed; it might be easier fer us to have our readin' time at night."

Missie nodded and settled down beside him. It was still light enough to see, but the light would not last for long. Willie found his place and began in an even voice.

"Fear thou not; for I am with thee: be not dismayed; for I am thy God: I will strengthen thee; yea, I will help thee; yea, I will uphold thee with the right hand of my righteousness."

"Yer pa underlined thet fer us. When he handed me the Bible he read it to me and marked it with this red ribbon. He said fer us to claim thet verse fer our own and to read it every day until we felt it real and meaningful in our hearts." [21–22]

When we let God's Word seep into our lives little
by little, crack by crack, it nourishes us and
becomes a part of us.

Man shall . . . live by . . . every word that proceedeth out of the
mouth of God.
MATTHEW 4:4

FEAR

Missie, are you ever scared?" Becky asked slowly.

"I didn't *think* I was." Missie hesitated. "Willie was so excited, an' I honestly thought that I wanted to go, too. An' I do—really, I do. But I didn't know—that I'd—well—that it'd hurt so much to leave Mama an' Pa. I didn't think that I'd feel so—empty. So now I'm beginnin' to feel scared."

"I'm glad thet I'm not the only one. I've never told anyone, not even John. I want so much for him to have his dream, but sometimes I fear thet I won't be able to make it come true fer him, thet my homesickness will keep him from bein' really happy. Do you think it ever gits better?"

"I truly hope so," Missie said. "I'm countin' on God to make it so."

"You know God? I'm so glad!" Becky exclaimed. "It's Him thet gives me daily courage, too. I'm not very brave—even *with* Him; but *without* Him I'd be a downright coward." [40–41]

God takes away only as many of our fears as we
give to Him.
What time I am afraid, I will trust in thee.
PSALM 56:3

WORSHIP

Sunday dawned clear and warm. The service had been set for 9:00 so that it would be over before the sun hung too hot in the sky. They began with a hearty hymn-sing, Henry leading in a clear baritone voice. Kathy Weiss taught the group a new song—simple and short but with a catchy tune. Many clapped their hands in accompaniment when they were not slapping mosquitoes. Mr. Weiss led the group in prayer with such fervor that Missie was reminded of home.

Then, one by one, people stood to thank God for His leading, for strength, for assurance in spite of fears, for incidents of protection along the way.

After the last volunteer speaker sat down, Willie read the Scripture. As the people left they thanked Henry for a job well done. Some suggested another hymn-sing round the fire that night, and so it was arranged.

The Sunday service and Sunday night hymn-sing became even more popular with the wagon-train members than the Saturday night doings. Missie and Willie were pleased to see the interest grow. The folks seemed to really need that restful time of worship and sharing on Sunday. [45–46]

> When we obey God's call to worship, He meets
> our need for rest.
> *Delight thyself also in the Lord. . . . Rest in the Lord.*
> PSALM 37:4–7

BUSYNESS

The countryside began changing. Missie tried to determine just what it was that made it seem so different—foreign—but it was hard to define. The trees were smaller and different than most of the trees she had been used to. The hills appeared different, too. Perhaps it was the abundance of short growth that clung to the sides of them. Whatever the difference, Missie realized that she was getting farther and farther from her home and those she loved. The now-familiar feeling of lonesomeness sometimes gnawed and twisted within her. Once in a while she was forced to bite her lip to keep tears from spilling down her cheeks. She must try harder, pray more. As she walked or worked she repeated to herself the blessed promise of Isaiah. Her greatest ally was busyness, and she tried hard to keep her hands and her mind occupied.   [48]

Busyness is an ally when it keeps away pain, but it
is an enemy when it keeps us away from God.

Mary . . . sat at Jesus' feet, and heard his word. But Martha was
cumbered about much serving. . . . And Jesus . . . said unto her,
Martha, Martha, thou art careful and troubled about many things: but
one thing is needful: and Mary hath chosen that good part.
LUKE 10:39–42

PROCRASTINATION

As Missie's body ached less, her spirit ached more. How she missed them—each one of them. How good it would be to feel her mama's warm embrace, or her pa's hand upon her shoulder. How she would welcome the teasing of Clare and Arnie or enjoy watching the growin' up of her younger sister, Ellie. And little Luke in his soft lovableness—how she ached to hug him again. "Oh, dear God," she prayed again and again, "please make me able to bear it."

With all of her strength, Missie fought to keep her feelings from Willie; but in so doing she didn't realize how much of her true self she was withholding from him. She often felt Willie's eyes upon her, studying her face. He fretted over her weariness and continually checked to be sure that she was feeling all right, was not overworking, was eating properly.

The truth was, Missie was not feeling well. Apart from her deep homesickness, there was nausea and general tiredness. But she didn't admit it to Willie. *It's not the right time yet. Willie would just worry,* she kept telling herself. But she sensed—and did not like—the strain between them.   [49]

Waiting for the "right time" may be an excuse for
doing the "wrong thing."
*Follow me. But he said, Lord, suffer me first to go and bury
my father.*
LUKE 9:59

THE WHOLE TRUTH

I been wantin' to tell you, but the time never seemed right," Missie said quietly. "Willie—we're gonna have a baby."

Willie stopped walking. "Ya aren't joshin'? An' yer sure?"

"Quite sure."

Willie stood silently for a moment, then shook his head. "I'm not sure thet wagon-trainin' an' babies go together."

"Oh, Willie, don't fuss. We'll be in our own place long before our baby ever arrives."

The look on Willie's face changed and he let out a whoop. Then he hugged Missie tight.

Suddenly Missie wanted to cry. It was such a joy to tell Willie, to see his exuberance, and to feel his strong arms about her. She had been wrong to withhold it from him.

"So this is why ya haven't been yerself. We gotta take better care of ya. I was so scared, Missie, thet maybe you'd changed yer mind—or thet maybe ya didn't even love me anymore—or thet ya had some bad sickness. I jest prayed an' prayed an' here—"

Missie had not realized what her homesickness had put Willie through. She must not hold back from him again. [53–54]

Trying to spare someone the worry of knowing the
truth may cause them more worry about what's
NOT true.

I have not concealed thy truth.
PSALM 40:10

ADVERSITY

As the day wore on, the intensity of the storm increased. The dark clouds overhead seemed angry as they poured water from a sodden sky. Soon the teams were straining to pull the heavy, high-wheeled wagons through the deepening mud.

The guides ranged back and forth, watching for trouble along the trail. It came all too soon. One of the lead wagons slid down a slippery, steep slope and hit a large rock. Wooden spokes snapped with a sickening sharpness. The wagon lurched and heaved but did not tip over. As soon as the last wagon was safely down the badly rutted hillside, Mr. Blake ordered a halt. It was useless to try to go on. The Big River would have to wait.

While Willie and Henry went to help the unfortunate Calley family, Missie wrapped a heavy shawl tightly about her and went in search of firewood. The other ladies and children were seeking dry material for their fires as well, and there was very little to be found. Missie felt cold and muddy and cross as she scrambled for bits and pieces of anything that might burn.

Only Mrs. Schmidt did not have to join the searchers. Her ever abundant supply of dry wood was unloaded from under the wagon seat. Missie wondered why she hadn't had the presence of mind to plan ahead as well.   [57–58]

Worrying about possible adversity is a waste of
energy; but preparing for it is not.

Gather all the food . . . [or] store . . . against the seven years of
famine.
GENESIS 41:35–36

EXPERIENCE

On the fifth day the sky began to clear, and the sun finally broke through on the dripping, miserable wagon train. The people, too, came out, stringing lines and hanging clothing and blankets to dry. The ground remained soggy. It could be days before the stands of water disappeared and even longer before the ground would be dry enough to allow the wagons to roll.

Missie felt somewhat like Noah as she descended from her wagon. Water was everywhere. How good it would be to see the dry land appear and the horses kick up dust. Oh, to be on the move again!

Mr. Blake felt impatient, too, but his many years on the trail told him that it would be useless to try to travel in the mud. They'd have to wait. Mr. Blake also knew that the rains of the past few days had made the Big River impossible to cross. But there was no need to pass this information on to the group. They'd take the problems one day at a time. [62–63]

Experience teaches us when to wait and when to
move forward.

I have learned by experience that the LORD hath blessed me for
thy sake.
GENESIS 30:27

HIDIN' THE HURT

The "town," as Mr. Blake feared, produced its casualties. A number of the men had been "out on the town." Most staggered in sometime during the night. Mrs. Kosensky took care of her husband with a cold bucket of water for his outside and hot coffee for his inside. Jessie Tuttle handled her driver-brother by stuffing him into the wagon and hitching the team herself.

Mrs. Thorne's husband failed to reappear at all. Mr. Blake eventually found him, and a livery wagon delivered him. Mrs. Thorne then picked up the reins of her team and maneuvered into position without giving her neighbors as much as a nod of apology for the three-hour delay. Nothing seemed to shake her from solid-rock indifference. Mrs. Thorne passed by Missie, her hands steady on the reins, her eyes unblinking against the glare of the sun. Missie almost missed it, but it was there—and what she saw made her stop short. Running down the coarse, tanned cheeks of the woman was a steady stream of tears. "Ya poor soul," Missie whispered. "Here ya are a-hurtin' an' nobody knows, so no one reaches out to you in understandin'. Oh, God, forgive me for not seein' past her stiff jaw to the hurts and the needs. Help me to show her kindness and love. She needs me. She needs *You*, Lord." [78–79]

A hard, crusty exterior may be hiding a tender,
needy soul.
And Peter remembered the words of Jesus. . . . And he went out,
and wept bitterly.
MATTHEW 26:75

When Willie returned from town, he started calling Missie before he reached the wagon. "I've found a place!" he almost whooped. Missie jerked to attention.

"A place for *what?*"

"For you," he declared, surprised at her question. "For you— while yer waitin' fer the baby."

Missie didn't tell him that she still didn't intend to *wait*. She intended to go. But she knew that it was useless to fight it.

"It's only one room—but it's a nice, fair size. An' it's with fine folks. I'm sure thet you'll like 'em, an' they even said that I can stay there, too, 'til the supply train is ready to leave. Mr. Taylorson runs a general store an' his wife teaches a bit of piano. Says ya might even learn to play the piano while yer a-waitin'."

"Oh, Willie!" Missie said in exasperation. "What in heaven's name would I want to learn piano for? What good would that do me?"

"It would help fill in the long hours," Willie interposed. "It might help a heap, iffen ya choose to let it." His words were mild but he gave her a searching look. [92]

Reprimands don't always have to be harsh.
A soft answer turneth away wrath.
PROVERBS 15:1

95

SOUL-WINNING

Y a know what I'm gonna miss most 'bout wagon-trainin'?" asked Henry. "I'm gonna miss the Sunday gatherin's."

"I guess I will, too," Missie said. "They were special, weren't they? An' you did a first-rate job, Henry. A real good job. Did you ever think of bein' a preacher?"

Henry's blush deepened. "I thought on it—sorta. But I ain't got what it takes to be a preacher. Very little book learnin' and not much civilizin' either."

"That's not true, Henry! You're a born leader. Didn't you notice how the people followed you, accepted you, expected you to take the lead?"

"They did, some," he agreed. "But thet was a wagon train, not a settlement church. There's a heap of difference there. I did decide one thing, though. I jest told the Lord thet iffen He had a place fer me—wherever it was—I'd be happy to do whatever I could. I don't expect it to be in a church, Missie—but there's lots of folks who need God who never come a-lookin' fer Him in a church."

"I'm glad, Henry," Missie said softly. "I'm glad you feel that way. And you're right; God needs lots of us—everywhere—to touch other people's hearts." [95–96]

Jesus didn't find His disciples in church.
Go out into the highways and hedges . . . and compel them to come in.
LUKE 14:23

ADJUSTMENT

Missie swallowed hard. Could a miracle take place just over the next hill? The land here was even more bleak than that around Tettsford Junction. Hills and more colorless hills, covered with coarse, dry-looking grass. Tumbleweed somersaulted along in the wind, rolling and bouncing forever. Occasional cactus plants or an outcropping of rocks were the only changes of scenery. They topped the hill and Willie reined in the horses. Missie shut her eyes, wishing she didn't have to open them.

"There it is. Ain't it somethin'? What d'ya think of it?"

Missie had been dreading that question. How could she answer it? She couldn't let Willie down—yet she couldn't lie. "It's—it's—really somethin'," she mumbled, thankful that she had remembered Willie's own words.

"Sure is," Willie agreed, interpreting her answer with his own optimism. Then he pointed out the bunkhouse, cookshack, barn, and house. They all looked like heaps of dried grass. "They're made of sod," Willie informed. "Ya pile up blocks of sod and it makes a real snug place to live in the winter."

No miracle had taken place "over the next hill." But Missie needed a miracle now—to help her adjust to what she knew lay ahead. [130–132]

Adjusting to circumstances is the first step in
overcoming them.

I have learned in whatsoever state I am, therewith to be content.
PHILIPPIANS 4:11

After the Christmas meal, Missie presented each one of the ranch hands with a pair of socks and woolen mittens. She was unprepared for their deep appreciation. For some it was their first Christmas gift since they were small boys. After the men had expressed their thanks, Missie began timidly, "Now I want to say thank you for your gift to me."

All eyes swung to her face. "I want to thank you," she said shyly, "for workin' so faithfully for my husband, for makin' his load—an' thus mine—easier, for not demandin' things that we can't provide." She hesitated, then smiled. "But most of all, I want to thank you for the good supply of chips for my fire that you didn't fuss 'bout haulin'. I've been thankful over an' over for those chips." Missie couldn't suppress a giggle. At that moment, Missie made friends for life. Not one of the men would have denied her anything in their power to provide.

After the men left, Willie gave Missie her gift, the most beautiful fruit bowl Missie had ever seen. Then he spoke softly. "Missie, I wonder iffen you'll ever know jest how happy ya made five people today? Those four cowpokes—an' *me.*"

Missie's eyes gleamed. "Then make it *six,* Willie—'cause in doin' what I could, the pleasure all poured right back on me. An' I got the biggest helpin' of happiness myself!" [145–147]

Giving happiness brings happiness.
It is more blessed to give than to receive.
ACTS 20:35

HONESTY

Shortly before daybreak, the herd grew restless. Then mayhem broke loose. By the time Henry and Clem realized the cause, a band of rustlers had driven off a large portion of the herd. Henry and Clem rode hard, but were able to cut back only the stragglers from the stampeding cattle. By the time the sleeping men heard the commotion, it was too late for them to assist.

After all the remaining cattle had been gathered, Willie's herd numbered only fifty-four head of full-grown cattle and thirty-two calves. Willie turned away, his shoulders slumped in defeat. He swallowed the lump in his throat and lifted his broad-brimmed hat to wipe the dust from his brow. The sick feeling in the pit of his stomach refused to leave. Could he get back on his feet? How long would it take? If he had been more patient and had worked for another year, he could have laid aside enough cash to cover such a tragedy. Now the only extra cash he had was the money for Missie's house. How could he ever tell her? Though he wished that he could keep the news from her, he knew it would be useless and untruthful to do so. She deserved to know the truth— even to know the seriousness of their situation. But Willie determined he would try to shield her from the pain and the fear that came with the knowing.   [151–152]

Accepting the truth is easier than living a lie.
We have a good conscience, in all things willing to live honestly.
HEBREWS 13:18

PROMISE

Willie presented Missie with the bleak facts as honestly and simply as he knew how. Missie ached for him. If only she could help him. Then, to her surprise, she heard him talking to the men about building the permanent ranch house. Missie waited until they were alone to mention it. "I overheard you discussin' with the hands your plans for buildin'. But, Willie, can we afford the house now, with the cattle losses an' all?"

"Thet changes nothin'. The money for the house has been set aside. Rebuildin' the herd'll jest have to wait."

"But if we don't have a herd, there won't be cattle to sell."

"There'll be some—eventually. An' I promised ya a house."

Missie knew she might later regret what she was about to say, but she had to say it: "Willie, I know you want to keep your promise—an' you will. But it could be postponed until we have the cattle to sell. If we stay in this house, just for now, and use the put-aside money to rebuild the herd, then next year we could build our house. The cattle are important to *me* too, you know."

Willie's jaw muscles tightened as if he was fighting for control. *Oh, God,* Missie prayed silently, *help me to support Willie in spite of what I want. Keep Your promise to uphold me now.* And He did.

The next thing she knew, Willie was pulling her close. He was accepting her gift. [152–153]

Only God can keep all His promises.
There hath not failed one word of all his good promise.
1 KINGS 8:56

A FRIEND

Missie's visitor was hardly more than a girl, with dusky skin, long, loose-flowing dark hair, and black eyes. Her full lips suggested laughter, and Missie felt drawn to her immediately, even though she could speak no English. There was so much that Missie wanted to talk about, to ask. But all they could do was play with Nathan, smile at one another, and sip tea.

When Maria indicated that she must go, Missie asked, in a primitive form of sign language, if they could pray together. Maria understood. "Si," she said, her face lighting up. She knelt beside her stool on the dirt floor of the shanty. Missie knelt too.

"Dear God," Missie began, "Thank You so much for sending Maria to me. Even though I can't talk to her, I can feel a friendship and warmth. May she be able to come again—soon, and may I be able to learn some of her words so that I can tell her how glad I am to have her. Thank You that we can pray together, and bless her now as she goes home. Amen."

Missie started to rise, but Maria's soft voice stopped her. It rose and fell, much like the sound of the gentle brook that ran by Missie's old home. Missie caught "Missee" and "Na-tan" in the flow of words and also recognized the "Amen." They rose together, smiling. Maria seemed to know Missie's God. Surely God himself had sent her. [165–166]

People we can pray with make the best friends.
Many were gathered together praying.
ACTS 12:12

HOME

Have you and Melinda set a wedding date?" Missie asked Henry. "Or am I bein' nosy?"

"Don't mind yer interest none. An' no, not yet. It depends on how soon I can build a house."

"With a little help, you can have a house up in a few days."

"I mean a *house*, Missie, not a sod shanty. I'd never ask Melinda to live in such conditions. "I saw the look in yer eyes when ya spotted the dirt floor, the dingy windows, the crowded—"

Missie stopped him. "Henry, do you see that look there now?"

Henry paused. "No," he said. "You've done well, Missie. An' I've admired ya fer it. But I won't ask thet of Melinda."

"I respect you for your thoughtfulness concernin' her, Henry. But you should know that I'd far sooner share this little one-room dirt dwellin' with Willie than to live in the world's fanciest house without him. An' I mean that."

Deep in her heart Missie marvelled at just how much she meant it. The truth unshackled her spirit from the small, shabby little dwelling to soar above it in the strength of her love for Willie. The long, dreaded winter no longer looked so frightening. They might be crowded, but they were bundled comfortably in the blanket of love. [186–187]

A house can keep bad weather out, but only a home can keep people in.
The LORD hath brought me home.
RUTH 1:21

CONGREGATION

The ranch hands, except Smith, no longer seemed reluctant to attend the Sunday services. At two o'clock they entered the house and took their places for the short time of singing, Bible reading, and prayer.

Missie thought that Rusty, the easy-going, open-hearted young boy of the group might want more than just a Sunday gathering. He eagerly sang the old hymns and listened attentively as the Scripture was read. But it was the shy, backward Lane who knocked on their door one evening and asked, in a stumbling voice, if the boss would mind explaining more about the Bible.

By the dim light of the flickering lamp, he and Willie went over the words of the Book. "If thou shalt confess with thy mouth the Lord Jesus, and shalt believe in thine heart that God hath raised him from the dead, thou shalt be saved."

Missie sat off to the side, finding jobs to do for which she needed little light. She prayed that God would bless His Word and open the understanding of the young man. God had been good to Willie and her. He had given them their own unique congregation. [190–191]

Buildings are nice for big gatherings, but they can't explain salvation to anyone.

In the name of our Lord Jesus Christ . . . ye are gathered together.
1 CORINTHIANS 5:4

ANGEL

Missie wasn't sure what wakened her, but she was sitting upright in bed, her blood pounding in her ears. Already Willie was springing from the bed.

"It's Nathan! He's chokin'!" Willie yelled. "Light the lamp."

"Oh, dear God, what can we do?" Missie cried, her heart tearing at each ragged breath of her small baby. *Oh, dear God, we need You now,* her heart cried. *Little Nathan Isaiah needs You now. Please, dear God, show us what to do, or send us someone who knows. Please, God.*

Missie rummaged through the medicines, having no idea what to look for. Suddenly there was a "hullo" outside the door. Without waiting for a reply, Cookie burst in. He did not ask questions. His eyes and ears had already taken in the answers.

"Croup!" he said explosively, and began giving orders.

Missie and Willie followed Cookie's directions throughout the night. Near morning, Cookie called out, "His breathin' is easin' some."

Missie looked at the little man who spoke as though he were used to working miracles. Touching his stubbled face she said, "Cookie Adams, you can't fool me. You're no grouchy, hard-ridin' ole cowpoke. You're a visitin' *angel.*" [196–200]

We may be surprised at whom God sends to answer

our prayers.

Some have entertained angels unawares.

HEBREWS 13:2

GROWING LOVE

W illie brought wonderful news today," Missie's mental letter said. "He says that the coming railroad will not only haul out cattle but will bring people as well. He says that you'll be able to come right on out here for a visit. I could hardly believe it at first, and now I can hardly wait. I never dreamed that I'd ever be able to show you my home." Missie realized that she had never before called this place home. "My home! It truly is! I don't feel the awful tug back east anymore—this is truly *my home*—mine an' Willie's. I can hardly wait to show 'em."

Missie turned to the sod shanty that had been her home for two years. "You know," she said to the building, "I'll miss you. I think I'll ask Willie to leave you sittin' here so I can come here an' think an' remember. I've done a heap of growin' since I entered this door—an' there's still more to do—I reckon."

It was hard to put her hopes and dreams on sheets of paper. It would be so much better to say, "Welcome to my home. There's love here. Love that started growin' way back on the farm an' traveled all the way here with us. *God's* love—just as He promised. *Your* love, for us as your children. And *our* love for one another and for our son. Love! That's what makes a home." [206–207]

A fancy house may not be the best place to grow
the best love.
The house of the righteous shall stand.
PROVERBS 12:7

LOVE'S ABIDING

JOY

IF ONLY

Marty's smile left her face, and her eyes misted as she thought of Missie. Oh, how she missed Missie! She had thought it was gradually supposed to get easier over the years of separation from loved ones, but it had not been so. With every part of her being Marty ached for Missie.

If only . . . if only, she caught herself thinking; *if only I could have one chat—if only I could see her again—if only I could hold her children in my arms—if only I could be sure that she is all right, is happy.* But the "if onlys" only tormented her soul. Marty was here. Missie was many, many days' journey to the west. Yet now she longed for her Missie. Though Missie was not bone of her bone nor flesh of her flesh—Missie being Clark and Ellen's daughter—Marty felt that Missie was hers in every sense of the word. The tiny baby girl with the pixie face who had stolen her heart and given life special meaning so many years ago was indeed *her* Missie. *Oh, how I miss you, little girl,* Marty whispered against the pane as a tear loosed itself and splashed down on the windowsill. *If only*— but Marty stopped herself. [13–14]

Dwelling on "if onlys" only increases our
dissatisfaction.

*Then said Martha unto Jesus, Lord, if thou hadst been here,
my brother had not died.*
JOHN 11:21

GIVING OURSELVES

Grandma Marty was given a chair of honor, and the birthday gifts began to arrive, carried in and presented by various hands. The children shared scraps of art work and pictures. Tina had even hemmed, by hand stitch, a new handkerchief. Nandry and Clae, presenting gifts from their families, laughed when they realized that they had gone together and purchased a new teapot, declaring that now she could "git rid of thet ol' one with the broken spout." Ellie's gift to her mother was a delicate cameo brooch, and Marty suspected that Clark had contributed largely to its purchase. Luke was last. His eyes showed both eagerness and embarrassment as he came slowly forward. It was clear that he was a bit uncertain as to how the others would view his gift.

"It didn't cost nothin'," he murmured.

"Thet isn't what gives a gift its value," Marty replied, both curious and concerned.

"I know thet you always said thet, but some folk—well—they think thet ya shouldn't give what cost ya nothin'."

"Ah," said Clark, seeming to realize what was bothering the boy, "but the cost is not always figured in dollars and cents. To give of yerself sometimes be far more costly than reachin' into one's pocket fer cash." [21]

Giving ourselves is the most costly gift, and the most valuable.

This is my body which is given for you.
LUKE 22:19

FIGHTING CIRCUMSTANCES

The next three days on the slow-moving train were difficult for Marty. Though still grateful for Clark's birthday gift—train tickets to visit Missie—she was in a fever to reach their daughter, and the many delays and the hesitant forward crawl irritated Marty. She was also tired from several nights without a good rest, and the train they rode was even less elegant than the first. The worn seats and cramped quarters made it difficult to sit comfortably, and there was no room for stretching or walking. The heat and the stuffiness of the passenger car almost overcame her, and bedbug bites did not help her frame of mind. Occasionally there was something of interest out of the train window, but usually there was nothing but brown hills and wind-swept prairie. Marty just wanted to get to Missie, and each time the train stopped and frittered away precious time, Marty chafed inside.

But all of her fretting did not get them one mile closer to Missie, Marty gradually came to realize. At length she willed herself to take a lesson from Clark and learn some patience. She settled herself in her corner and determined not to stew. She even decided to study the countryside and see what it might have to share with her. [59–60]

When we fight our circumstances, rather than make peace
with them, the circumstances inevitably win.
*Wait on the LORD: be of good courage, and he shall strengthen
thine heart.*
PSALM 27:14

MORE THAN MORTAR

The last stop of Missie's tour of the ranch was the little sod shanty. Marty gazed from the sod roof to the packed-dirt floor. *This is the "home" that waited for you after that long, hard trip?* Marty thought. *Ya actually lived in this little shack—an' with a baby! How could ya ever do it? How could ya stand to live in such a way? My, I . . ."*

But Missie was speaking: "Willie wanted to tear it down, to get it out of here, but I wouldn't hear tell. Got a lot of memories, this little place. We've had to re-sod the roof a couple of times. Roofs don't last too long with the winter storms, the wind an' rain; an' once they start to leak, they aren't good for anything."

Marty did not express her feeling about the soddy. Instead she expressed her feeling for her girl. "I'm so proud of you, Missie— so proud. Ya looked beyond these here dirt walls into the true heart of the home. Home ain't fancy dishes an' such, Missie. Home is love and carin'." Marty's hand touched her daughter's cheek. "Ya made a home with jest yer own hands an' yer own heart. I'm proud of ya. So very proud."

Marty looked around once more before leaving the small sod shack; this time it did not look as bleak, nor the floor as earthy. In those few short minutes something had happened that changed the appearance of the little room. [69–70]

Love can change the way we see things.
We look not at the things which are seen, but at the things which are not seen: for the things which are seen are temporal; but the things which are not seen are eternal.
2 CORINTHIANS 4:18

TUNNEL OF SUFFERING

An' the Marshalls? How are they doin'?" asked Missie, eager to catch up on news of people back home.

"It's sad," Marty answered, "sad to see the Marshalls an' their son, but it's beautiful, too. There is so much love there. Rett is a very loving child. He's a young man really, but he is still a child. Wanda and Cam really love 'im. He is so good with animals thet it's 'most uncanny. Wild or tame—they all seem to understand Rett."

"An' Wanda's happy?"

"Happy? Yah, she's happy. She needs to rely on her God daily, though. She has her hard times, but I'm sure thet she wouldn't be tradin' her boy fer all the boys in town."

Missie shook her head as she thought of the grief that Wanda had carried. "She has suffered so much," she said softly.

"Yah," acknowledged Marty, "she has suffered—suffered and growed. Sometimes it seems to take the one to bring the other."

"When one does suffer, it is good to see that it hasn't been wasted—that the sufferer allows God to make it a blessin' rather than a bitterness," Missie expressed.   [75–76]

From the tunnel of suffering we have a choice
of two exits—bitterness and blessing.
*For our . . . affliction . . . worketh for us a far more exceeding and
eternal weight of glory.*
2 CORINTHIANS 4:17

MAKING MEMORIES

Oh, Mama," Missie said, "I've longed for you so often. I promised the Lord that I'd be content with seein' you, an' here I've been upset because you can't stay longer. I'm ashamed of myself. We'll just make every minute count. We'll fill our time with so much happiness that we'll have barrels of memories to keep us when the time comes that we need to part again."

Marty smoothed Missie's hair. "Thet sounds like a grand idea," she said. "I've tucked away a few of these precious memories already."

Missie stood up. "Well," she said, "let's just get on with another one. Willie has developed a real liking for popcorn before bed, so let's go pop us some. He says that there just isn't anything better than to have a close family chat over popcorn. It's warm, an' homey, an' fillin'." Missie laughed and led the way to the big kitchen. [77]

One of the best parts of growing old is enjoying all
the pleasant memories we've taken time to
store up.
The righteous . . . shall still bring forth fruit in old age.
PSALM 92:12, 14

DOUBTS

Y ou must pray for us," Maria said in response to Missie's comment that they'd been missing Juan and Maria at the Sunday meetings. "Juan has many doubts, many questions," she continued. "He cannot leave the church of his past, but he has here no church of his own. He does not want his child to grow up without the proper church teaching, but he is no longer sure what he wants him taught. There was much about Juan's church that he did not agree with, but he loved his church. He has not forsaken it. He will never forsake it. In the services at your house we have heard new and strange things from the Bible. We did not know of them before. It takes much wisdom, much time, much searching of the heart to know the truth. Please be patient with us, Missie. And please pray for us that we may know the truth. One day we think, 'This is it,' and the next day we say, 'No, that is it.' It is hard—so very hard."

"I understand," said Missie. "We will pray. We will pray that you will find the truth—not that you will believe as we believe, but that you will find the truth." [87]

We should be more concerned about helping
people find God than helping them find our church.

Those that seek me early shall find me.
PROVERBS 8:17

PRAYER

Marty and Missie numbly went about their task. Neither talked, although both were troubled with thoughts that would not be stilled. They worked in silence until Marty noticed Missie fighting back the tears. She went to her and took her in her arms.

"He'll be all right. God won't let anythin' happen to 'im. He'll be fine." Oh, how Marty wanted to believe her own words! *They have to be true. They just have to. If anything happens to Clark . . .* Her arms tightened around Missie and she began to pray aloud.

"God, Ya know how we need Ya now. Ya know how we love Clark, and thet he loves You, Lord. An' now we're askin' thet Ya help him recover from the terrible accident in the mine. Thet Ya give 'im back his mind an' body, iffen it be Yer will, Lord. Amen."

"Oh, Ma!" Missie cried, "don't pray like that. *Of* course it be His will. He's gotta heal 'im. He's gotta."

"Yer pa always prayed, 'Yer will be done.' "

"You can pray thet iffen ya want to," said Missie, "but I'm gonna tell God exactly what I want. I want Pa well agin. What's wrong with tellin' God jest what ya want Him to do?"

"Yer pa says thet we don't be orderin' God; we ask." [111]

If all we do in prayer is tell God what we want, we
reduce Him to the role of servant and elevate
ourselves to the position of master.

*[Jesus] . . . prayed, saying, O my Father, if it be possible, let this
cup pass from me: nevertheless not as I will, but as thou wilt.*
MATTHEW 26:39

DISGUISED BLESSING

Marty lifted herself to her feet and took the cup of coffee. She was surprised at how stiff she had become. She wondered how long she had been there beside Clark. Missie pushed a chair toward her and she sat down.

"Willie still isn't back. Don't know why he—"

"Maybe he went fer a doctor," Marty interrupted. "He said thet yer pa's leg—"

"I'm afraid there's no doctor anywhere around," Missie offered sadly. "He might have heard of someone good at setting breaks, though."

"Willie said if we needed anything to call the men. He also said not to let Pa stir around none. Might hurt his leg."

Marty looked at the motionless Clark. "Looks like we needn't worry none 'bout thet. Wish he *would* stir some. It would make me feel some better iffen I could jest talk to him."

"Maybe it's a blessin' thet he has thet bump on his head. At least he doesn't suffer as much. By the time he comes to again, maybe the pain will be cared fer some."

Marty hadn't thought of the unconsciousness as a blessing, but perhaps it was.   [113–114]

Blessings sometimes show up in unrecognizable
disguises.
The LORD thy God turned the curse into a blessing.
DEUTERONOMY 23:5

WONDERING WHY

Clark remained unconscious the entire next day. Marty stayed by his bed, longing to be able to talk with him. Missie came as often as her duties would allow. In the late afternoon, Willie returned to the house and insisted that both of the ladies take a rest. After a bit of an argument, they went. They realized that they could not carry on longer without some sleep. Willie had Wong bring him coffee, and he settled himself beside Clark's bedside. He had slept very little himself in the last two days. His eyelids felt heavy and his eyes scratchy. He rubbed a calloused hand over his face.

Why did this have to happen? Why? The time they had looked forward to for so long—had dreamed of as a time of joyous reunion—had turned into a nightmare. *Why?* Surely God hadn't brought Clark and Marty way out here to take Clark's life and destroy Marty's faith? It was all a puzzle to Willie. [118]

The small question why? requires an answer as
big as God.
My God, my God, why hast thou forsaken me?
MATTHEW 27:46

HEALING

Marty went to the sickroom occasionally, but Clark's misery was more than she could bear. At last, she went to her room again and fell beside her bed. This time she didn't pray for her husband's healing.

"Oh, God!" she cried. "Ya know best. I can't stand to see 'im suffer so. I love 'im, God, but iffen Ya want to take 'im, then it's all right. I won't be blamin' Ya, God. Ya know what's best. I don't want 'im to suffer, God. I leave 'im in Yer hands. Yer will be done, whether it's healin' or takin', thet's up to You, God. An', God, whatever Yer will, I know thet Ya'll give me—an' all of us—the strength thet we need to bear it."

Marty arose from her knees and went to find Missie. She still shivered with each scream from Clark, but Marty knew that God was in control and that His divine will would be done.

"Missie," Marty said, taking the girl into her arms. "It's gonna be all right. I know it is."

Missie wiped her tears on her apron and straightened up just as someone knocked on the door. Maria stood there, her shoulders square and her eyes shining with faith and pride. And just behind her stood Juan. "Can we come in?" she asked. "My husband . . . is a doctor."

[128–130]

> God can heal in at least two ways: making us
> better or taking us home.
> *So now also Christ shall be magnified in my body, whether it*
> *be by life, or by death.*
> PHILIPPIANS 1:20

LOSS

Clark's face went white as Marty talked. The words *gangrene* and *poison* seemed to linger in his eyes. "An' yer sayin'—?"

"I'm sayin' thet Dr. De la Rosa fixed yer leg as best he could— in the only way he could. He took it off, Clark. He took it off 'fore it killed ya."

Clark turned away his face. Marty saw a shiver vibrate all through him. She threw her arms around him and held him close. "Clark," she said, "I know thet isn't what ya wanted to hear. I know thet ya didn't want to lose a leg. I didn't want it either, Clark. With my whole bein', I fought it. But it was yer leg or *you.* Fer a while, it looked like it would be both. Oh, Clark, I'm jest so thankful to God thet He sent a doctor along in time to spare ya. I don't know how I'd ever made it without ya, Clark. God spared ya, an' I'm so glad. We'll git by without the leg . . . I promise."

Clark smoothed her hair and held her close. His trembling eventually stopped. He could even speak. "Yer right. It'll be all right. Guess it jest takes some gettin' used to. I can still be a-carin' fer my family. One leg ain't gonna make a lot of difference. Iffen the Lord hadn't a figured thet I could do without thet there leg, He wouldn't have 'llowed this, now would He?" [138–139]

God never takes away anything we need to do His will.
*Look to yourselves, that we lose not those things which we
have wrought, but that we receive a full reward.*
2 JOHN 8

Juan entered Clark's room, his pulse racing. He remembered the time his brother had discovered his missing limb. Juan didn't blame any man for taking the news hard.

"I heard thet I owe ya my life," Clark said. "It must be a powerful hard decision fer a man to make—to take a man's limb an' spare the man's life, or let him die with both legs on. I want to tell ya 'thank you' for bein' brave enough to make the choice fer me when I wasn't able to make it fer myself. I would have chosen to live, Juan. Life is good—an' life is in the hands of Almighty God. I'm not sayin' thet I fancy learnin' to live without a leg. I'm not pretendin' to be some hero thet it won't bother none. But I am sayin' 'thank you' fer givin' me thet chance. With God's help, I'll make it. If He 'llowed it, then He must have a plan to git me through it, too. Fer He plans only for my good."

Juan watched Clark without speaking. There were no angry cries, no cursing, no incriminations. There was a distinct difference here between the way this man accepted his handicap and the way his brother had. Juan determined to do some thinking about what made the difference. One thing he already knew— where his own brother had cursed God, this man thanked God. Perhaps it had something to do with that. [139—140]

How we respond to tragedy reveals how we have responded to God.

Then said [Job's] wife unto him, . . . Curse God and die. . . . But . . . in all this Job did not sin.
JOB 2:9–10

FACING THE FUTURE

I don't be pretendin' thet the news about my leg hasn't shook me up a bit," Clark said to Dr. De la Rosa. "It's gonna take some thinkin' on to git used to the idea. I don't much feel up to thinkin' at the moment. Ya happen to have somethin' to help a man git a little sleep instead? I think thet it might be easier to handle come mornin'."

Dr. De la Rosa moved to prepare some medication.

Clark did not go to sleep immediately. He spent time thinking, even though he wished that he could shove the whole problem off to the side and pretend that it did not exist. He also did some praying—deep, soul-searching praying—asking for God's help in the hours of adjustment and growing. He even did some weeping—heart-rending weeping—with sobs that shook his large frame. When it was all over, he wiped away the tears from his gaunt cheeks, set his chin, and reached for the unseen hand of God.   [140—141]

> The only safe way to walk into the future is with
> Someone who has already been there.
> *I am Alpha and Omega, the beginning and the ending,*
> *saith the Lord, which is, and which was, and which is to come.*
> REVELATION 1:8

STRANGE TALK

The two families from town whose boys had been involved in the old mine accident came out to the LaHaye farm for a visit. The ladies, still unable to talk of the incident without weeping, thanked Clark over and over for saving their sons. Though it was difficult for them to truly express what they were feeling, they tried to make Clark understand how sorry they were that he had lost his leg. Clark assured them that in every circumstance of his life—whether good or bad—he believed with all of his heart that God knew his situation and was more than able to help him through it. He told them he was aware that there would be adjustments and some of them would be difficult; but, though *he* was human, *God* was sovereign. The visitors looked a trifle uneasy at Clark's "strange talk." Marty, watching with understanding eyes, supposed it was as new to them as it had been to her when she had first joined Clark's household so many years before. Clark's face and voice held such confidence that the people in the room, in spite of their doubts, were sure he meant every word. [147–148]

When we talk with God regularly, we pick up
a vocabulary that is foreign to people who don't
know Him.

All that heard [Jesus] were astonished at his understanding and answers.
LUKE 2:47

TACT

Willie turned to Andy's parents. "We'd be most happy to have ya join us for the Sunday meetin's, too," he said.

The man was quick to dismiss the idea. He shook his head and shuffled his feet. "Don't think thet we be a-needin' thet," he mumbled. "Our boy is jest fine now. Doc set his ankle and it's most as good as new."

Willie held his tongue. He wished to say that one did not go to church only when one had an apparent need, but now did not seem the proper time to say it. Clark said it—but in a little different way.

"We spend a bit of time in our service thanking the Lord as well. Perhaps you an' yer wife would like an opportunity to thank God thet He 'llowed yer boy to git out safely. Ya would be welcome to join us at any time—fer any reason." [149]

When a word of admonition is called for, we
should make it kind, not critical.
A word fitly spoken is like apples of gold.
PROVERBS 25:11

PRIDE

Clark nodded. "I understand. A man does have his pride. 'Course a man can, with God's help, swaller his pride an' do what he knows he should. Iffen yer mother is livin', I'm sure thet she is hurtin' too. She has no idea iffen yer alive or dead. An' iffen yer father is still livin' an' has maybe changed his feelin's some, how would he ever be findin' ya to let ya know?"

Still Juan struggled with the issue. "You do not know—" he began.

"No," agreed Clark, "I do not know. I'm admittin' to thet. But God does, an' I don't think thet *you're* admittin' to thet. Shore thing, I wasn't raised as you was raised, but things have been a bit tough fer me at times, too. Life can be pretty quick to take a swipe at a man. Sometimes we can't duck the blows. We jest gotta take 'em head-on. They smart a bit, to be sure. But God knows all thet. He not only knows, but He cares. He doesn't ask from us thet we *understand* or even *like* what we face, but jest thet we face it like a man, an' do what we know to be right, regardless of the fact thet it goes against us at times. God can help us do the right thing—even though it seems impossible." [152–153]

Chewing on pride doesn't make it easier
to swallow.
In the mouth of the foolish is a rod of pride.
PROVERBS 14:3

MIRACLES

I knew as soon as I seed yer leg thet only a miracle could save it," Cookie said. "An' seems to me we been a little short on miracles in my lifetime."

Clark smiled. "I ain't seen an over-abundance of miracles myself, but I shore ain't doubtin' them none." Watching Cookie's expectant face, Clark went on. "Guess one of the biggest miracles thet I know of is when God takes a no-good sinner and makes a saint fittin' fer heaven outa 'im. Even an earthly fella can put a messed-up body together agin. But only God can restore a crushed and broken soul. Yessir, *thet's* a miracle. Take me now," Clark said. "When I first woke up to the fact thet I only had one leg, a part of me died inside. I started tellin' myself how sorry I could be fer myself, an' even how God had let me down. My body was broken, an' my soul wanted to sympathize with it. My soul wanted to curl up an' hurt an' suffer an' become bitter an' ugly. Now, God didn't choose to do a miracle on this here leg, but He did a bigger an' more important miracle. He worked over the inner me—the soul of me. Thet's where I needed the miracle the most, so thet's where He applied His amazin' power. In here," said Clark, pointing to his broad chest, "in here, I don't hurt anymore." [154–155]

A miraculously healed body lasts for a lifetime; a miraculously healed soul lasts for eternity.

The water that I shall give him shall be . . . a well of water springing up into everlasting life.

JOHN 4:14

MAKING GOOD

Henry came directly to the point. "Been thinkin' lately," he said. "We really need some preachin' at our Sunday meetin's. We read the Bible together, but some of these folks need someone to explain what it's meanin'."

"Sounds good to me," responded Clark. "Ya got any plans?"

"Yah," said Henry, "been thinkin' on you. Ya been studyin' the Bible fer years. An' you've heard lots of preachin'. An ya believe the Holy Spirit can teach the truth. An' ya ain't overly busy these days, are ya?"

Clark chuckled. "No," he said. "Been makin' a few tops an' whistles, an' tying a few knots, an' eatin', an' complainin', an' makin' folks run around waitin' on me." He paused. "Come to think on it, seems I been powerful busy after all."

When they stopped laughing Henry said, "Well, will ya do it?"

"I'll need to think an' pray 'bout thet one," Clark answered.

"You do thet," encouraged Henry, feeling quite confident where Clark's thinking and praying would lead him.

Clark continued working on his crutch while he thought about the conversation. Maybe God could turn this whole tragic accident into something good. [157–158]

> Whenever anything bad happens we can start
> watching to see how God will use it for good.
> *All things work together for good to them that love God,*
> *to them who are the called according to his purpose.*
> ROMANS 8:28

ANSWERED PRAYER

Juan stopped to visit Clark after being away for three weeks. The LaHayes had been informed that Juan and Maria had gone away, and everyone assumed that Juan was still gathering equipment and supplies for his medical practice. He greeted Clark now with a firm handshake and clear eyes. Marty sensed that he wanted to talk to Clark in private and left the two of them alone over steaming cups of coffee.

"Well, I have been home," Juan said with deep feeling.

"I'm glad," said Clark. "An' how did yer pa receive you?"

Juan's eyes clouded. "My father, I am sorry to say, was not there to greet me. He died seven months ago."

"I'm sorry, " Clark said.

"I am sorry, too. I should have gone sooner. I should not have let my stubborn pride keep me away."

"An' yer mother?"

"My mother welcomed me with outstretched arms. My father's death left my mother all alone. Daily she prayed that if her son Juan was still living he would come back to her. Because of my foolishness, it took a long time for my mother's prayers to be answered." [171–172]

God's answers to our prayers may be delayed by
someone's stubbornness or pride.
Pride compasseth them about as a chain.
PSALM 73:6

WORSHIP

Senora De la Rosa was a delicate, dark-complexioned woman with flashing eyes and a quick smile. In spite of her years and the intense sorrow in her past, she still had a youthful spirit and vibrant outlook on life. Clark and Marty liked her immediately.

"My mother had no desire to live alone on the rancho," Juan explained. "As I did not wish to return to ranching in that area, we decided to sell the ranch to the man who has run it for my father. Mother is insisting on using much of the money from the sale for my medical practice. She wants us to have good equipment for those who need help. She is going to live with us. We are all so happy. Maria's mother died when she was a very young girl. We are all very happy, Mr. Clark, and we thank you."

"Mama has said that we shall all come to service together," said Maria. "When God works to answer her prayers through people who worship—even though they worship in a different way than she is used to—they must have the approval of God, she says. And so God would also surely approve of us worshiping together with them. So we shall be here next Sunday—and all the Sundays—and we will be glad to help in the building of the new church." [173–174]

Whom we worship is more important than how we worship.
Thou shalt have no other gods before me.
EXODUS 20:3

IMPATIENCE

Cookie dropped in to see Clark often. Clark did not discuss with Marty much of their conversation, but Marty realized that the old cowboy was troubled about his past life and its effect on his future. Marty wanted to hasten "the awakening" and say outright to Cookie, "So yer a sinner an' ya realize thet yer bad deeds can keep ya from heaven. I was a sinner, too. But one needn't stay in thet state. Christ Jesus came so thet every person could be forgiven and restored to all that God intended when He created us. All ya need do, Cookie, is to accept the gift of life that He offers to ya. It's jest thet simple. Nothin' to it at all. No need to be a-frettin' an' a-stewin' over whether it be a good idea or a bad idea. Common sense tells ya thet ya can't lose on such a deal. Jest do it an' git it taken care of."

Clark was far more patient with the man and explained carefully what Scripture had to say about the original fall into sin and selfishness, man's need of a Savior, and God's solution to this need. Cookie was gradually realizing his need and understanding what Christ had done for him. Clark felt confident that when Cookie made his decision, there would be no turning back. Still, Marty inwardly chafed, wishing it wouldn't take him so long.

[177–178]

When we push people to make important
decisions, we may unwittingly encourage them to
make the wrong one.
He that is hasty of spirit exalteth folly.
PROVERBS 14:29

FAITH

Lane, the cowboy who had helped Doc De la Rosa with Clark's surgery, was growing spiritually. He read the Bible daily and tried to live by its commands and concepts. Lane could never be accused of being a hypocrite. Even the bitter Smith began to show a grudging respect for Lane. One day Smith admitted to Jake, "Don't hold much to religion. Always figured thet it was fer women an' kids an' men who couldn't stand on their own feet; but iffen I was ever to git religion, I'd want the kind thet Lane got."

"So where did Lane git his special brand?" sneered Jake.

"Reckon he got it from the same place thet the boss an' his pa-in-law got theirs. It seems to be made of the same stuff."

Jake thought of Willie and his steadiness even through the tough times, his fairness with his men, and his concern for his community. He also thought of Clark and his acceptance of his handicap, and he murmured under his breath, "Yah, reckon it is." Then he turned to Smith. "So, iffen they are so anxious to share it, what's stoppin' ya from gittin' yerself some?"

Smith just scowled and rode away. [178–179]

When it comes to faith, no one has a good answer to Jake's question: "What's stoppin' ya from gittin' yerself some?"
Through faith [they] subdued kingdoms, wrought righteousness, obtained promises, stopped the mouths of lions. . . .
HEBREWS 11:33

LAST CHANCE

P lease, Doc," said Clark, "iffen there is anything ya can be doin' to bring him through—I'll stand the bill. This here is the father of two girls thet Marty an' me raised as our own. He's been bullheaded and stubborn, thoughtless and sometimes cruel, but his girls love 'im. Iffen only Jedd can live long enough fer someone to tell 'im of God's love an' fergiveness. I jest can't bear the thought of 'im dyin' without my bein' able to talk with 'im 'bout his girls and 'bout God's love fer 'im."

Dr. De la Rosa looked very solemn. "I can only try," he said. "You pray that God might work a miracle."

Clark knelt beside Jedd's bed. "Dear God," he began, "Ya knew this here man before us. He's been sinful, God, but so have we all. He's made some bad judgments, but so have we. He needs Ya, Lord, just as we all do. He has never recognized Ya as God an' Savior, an' he needs thet chance, Lord. He can't hear or respond, so we need Ya to do a miracle, Lord, an' help the doc to bring 'im round so thet we can talk with 'im and read Yer Word so thet he might have thet chance to decide. We are askin' this Lord, in the name of Jesus, Yer Son, who died thet each one of us— includin' Jedd here—could have life eternal. Thank ya, Lord, fer hearin' the prayer of those who bow before Ya. Amen." [186]

Everyone gets a last chance to accept God, but
none of us knows when it will be.

Now is the accepted time. . . . Now is the day of salvation.
2 CORINTHIANS 6:2

Clark put his arm around his wife and pulled her close. "Those girls of ours are gonna be happy to know thet their pa joined their ma today. Jedd Larson made his peace with his Savior." Clark cleared his throat. "But he joined Tina in another way, too. Jedd didn't make it," Clark said quietly. "Juan had to do surgery. Jedd wasn't strong enough to stand it. The frozen fingers and toes had turned bad; there wasn't any way thet Juan could save 'im. He's been stayin' with 'im day an' night, fightin' to bring 'im through this but—"

"But he did, Clark. He did!" exclaimed Marty. "Because of Juan's fight to save 'im, Jedd not only has life—but *everlastin'* life."

"I'm afraid thet a doctor doesn't look at things thet way," said Clark soberly.

"But it's true. And, oh, Clark, iffen you hadn't been here, Jedd maybe wouldn't have decided to make his peace with God 'fore he died." Marty's eyes fell to Clark's pant leg, pinned up securely just below the knee. "Iffen it wouldn't have been fer the accident, ya wouldn't have been here, Clark. We would have been gone home long ago." [195–196]

God may take extreme measures to put us where
He wants us.

[Joseph's brothers] cast him into a pit. . . . And the Midianites sold him into Egypt. . . . And Pharaoh said unto Joseph, . . . Thou shalt be over my house . . . only in the throne will I be greater than thou.
GENESIS 37:24, 36; 41:39, 40

CURIOSITY

On the day set for the church-building bee wagons loaded with food, tools, and excited families headed for the Newtons' ranch. Juan had discovered two experienced carpenters from town who took charge of the actual construction. The neighborhood men offered their hands wherever they were needed.

Within the week, the church building was lifting its spire proudly toward the sky, the barren prairie and wide horizon making a dramatic silhouette. Senora De la Rosa wept the first time she heard the bell peal, reaching across the miles without even echoing from the distant hills.

Many new faces appeared in the congregation for the first service in the new church. Marty sat with Missie and her family on one of the new pews. *While we've been here,* Marty thought, *God has provided a doctor for their bodies' needs and a church for their spiritual needs. Thank Ya, Lord!*

Clark wondered, as he looked over the crowd, how many were there for social reasons or idle curiosity and how many were true worshipers "in spirit and in truth." Regardless of their purpose, he saw a real opportunity to open the Word of God to them.

[199—200]

Curiosity may be a person's first step toward choosing a Christ-filled eternity.
And the keeper of the prison . . . said, Sirs, what must I do to be saved?
ACTS 16:27, 30

CHRIST IN US

How did you an' Cookie make out?" asked Missie, knowing that Clark had been looking for an opportunity for a heart-to-heart talk with Cookie about his relationship with God.

"We had a good talk—nice an' open—but Cookie is still hesitant. He says thet he wants to be sure he is acceptin' Jesus Christ—not Clark Davis."

"I don't understand," said Missie.

"Well," said Clark modestly, "Cookie says thet he admires me—guess 'cause both of us had the same kind of accident. Not much to admire a man fer, but Cookie reasons a little different than some men do. Anyway, he listens to the Word as I give it Sunday by Sunday; he sees me able to make do with one leg—I don't know. He's got it all mixed up as to what I can do as a man and what I can do with the Lord's help. He's not sure yet where the difference lies. Cookie's right, ya know. I don't want him to be a follower of Clark Davis. Iffen he can't find the difference here, then he should wait until he does. No good followin' me. Nothin' thet I can give to Cookie thet he can't find in hisself."

[201–202]

> People should be able to see Christ *in* us, but we
> need to be careful that they not see us
> *instead* of Christ.

I am crucified with Christ: nevertheless I live; yet not I, but Christ liveth

in me.

GALATIANS 2:20

LOVE'S UNENDING

LEGACY

CONTROL

Marty laughed a tight little laugh that caught in her throat. *See,* she wanted to say to her gathered family, *nothin' has changed— not really—at least nothin' thet really matters.* But perhaps they all got the message without her saying anything, for Marty noticed the changing expressions on the faces before her—first the pain, then the acceptance, and finally the relief.

Pa was still Pa. His accident had not altered his character. He was still in command. Oh, not of incidents, maybe; but he was in command of himself. He had not let a missing leg shape who he was, the person he had become. He was still in control. No, that was not right. Clark had never claimed to be in control. That was the secret. The man who stood before them, the man they were lucky enough to call "Pa," the one they had loved and respected and learned early to obey, had always assured them that the secret to life and its true meaning was not to try to take over the controls. The answer to a life of meaning and deep peace was to always leave the controls well in the hand of the Almighty Father. And the fact that *He* was still totally and wisely in control not a one of them in the close little circle doubted.   [17]

> The only way to take control is to give it up.
> *Whosoever will lose his life for my sake shall find it.*
> MATTHEW 16:25

CHANGELESSNESS

Down the path Marty walked until she could hear the soft gurgle of the spring. She bent to touch the shimmering coolness of the stream as it whispered its way across the smooth stones that formed the bottom. Then she lowered herself to the ground and reached out to trail a hand in the water. It was cold—so cold that it made her fingers cramp. Marty marveled at the miracle of the cold spring water. Where did it come from? What kept it so cold? She sat still, watching the swiftly flowing water. A woodpecker hammered on a nearby tree. A wood mouse scurried through the grass. Marty watched a dragonfly dip and swirl over the creek waters. She continued her silent vigil, listening and watching.

Marty loved the woods. It was such a refreshing place, and she needed refreshing. Physically she was still bone-weary from the long trip home. Emotionally she was drained from the excitement of rejoining her family and exploring her beloved home and farm. She had made many adjustments over the last year. She knew that life was full of adjustments; to live meant to change. But today Marty thanked the Lord for the things that stayed constant in a changing world—even things as simple as a quiet stream and a gurgling spring. [28–29]

Change makes life interesting; changelessness
makes it meaningful.

He changeth the times and the seasons. . . . I am the LORD, I
change not.
DANIEL 2:21; MALACHI 3:6

SURPRISE

I've made an appointment with Dr. Watkins," Clark stated matter-of-factly. Marty's head jerked up, concern filling her eyes.

"Ain't ya been feelin' okay? Is yer leg—?"

"Ain't fer me. It's fer you. I've been worryin' 'bout ya. Thought thet it might jest take a while fer ya to get back on yer feet like, but ya haven't, Marty. Ya still have to push yerself an'—"

"Wish ya hadn't done thet," Marty broke in. "Nothin' wrong with me." Then suddenly she began to cry.

Fear gripped Clark's heart. Was something seriously wrong? "Please, God, please not," he whispered. "Somethin' is wrong, isn't it?" he finally managed.

Marty nodded.

"What is it, Marty? What are ya expectin'—?" Clark couldn't finish. He wasn't sure he wanted to hear.

"A baby," she cried.

"A *baby*? Oh, Marty," Clark said, giving her a little shake.

Marty looked at Clark. There was neither reproach nor pity on his face. But there was love. Lots of love. Marty flung her arms tightly about his neck. "You're not upset?"

"Why would I be upset? Here I was a-worryin' about our last child movin' away, an' God is a-sendin' us another!" [43–45]

God meets our needs in unexpected ways.

Sarah conceived, and bare Abraham a son in his old age. . . .
And Sarah said, God hath made me to laugh, so that all that
hear will laugh with me.
GENESIS 21:2, 6

HEAVEN

Without comment Clark helped Marty into the wagon. Arnie placed the wrapped brick at her feet and tucked a heavy robe securely about her. Clark picked up the reins, clucked to the team, and they were off.

On the long, silent trip to the Grahams' Marty tried to accept the truth that Ben Graham was dead—but it did not seem real. A million stars seemed to blink overhead. She wondered if anyone knew just how many were up there. No, she supposed not. There were too many to be numbered. Only God himself knew the actual count.

And God himself knows about each one of His children. Marty closed her eyes. He knew her heart. He knew of Ben. He had already welcomed Ben into the courts of heaven. Was He glad . . . pleased to have one more child at home? Marty would be. If one of her far-off children were suddenly to walk through her door, she would be celebrating. Maybe God was celebrating—celebrating because Ben was home. [67]

Having loved ones in heaven makes us more eager
to get there.

In my Father's house are many mansions: . . . I go to prepare a
place for you. And . . . I will come again, and receive you unto
myself; that where I am, there ye may be also.
JOHN 14:2–3

MEANING

Marty toyed with an edge of the table. "Wouldn't hurt none iffen ya tried to look ahead," she said. "Christmas is comin'. Ya got a whole passel of grandchildren. Got their gifts all ready?"

Ma shook her head. "Oh, Marty, I jest have no heart fer Christmas!"

Marty laid a hand on the shoulder of the older woman. "The hardest Christmas I ever faced was the one jest after I lost Clem," she stated. "But ya know what? In lookin' back now, I see it as my most meanin'ful Christmas. I think maybe it was because thet year I decided to use Christmas as a growin' time. I didn't even understand what it was all 'bout at the time, but I knew thet God had a far deeper meanin' fer Christmas than we usually give it. I wanted to find an' understand thet meanin'. At the time, all I knew was thet I wanted to give Missie a special Christmas. She had already lost so much, an' I wanted to help heal some of those painful memories. In givin' to Missie, I got far more myself. I kinda think thet's the true meanin' of Christmas. Now ya got a family thet ya love very much. They are all hurtin' in their own way, but mostly they are hurtin' fer you. Christmas ain't gonna mean much to any of 'em—'less *you* can give it meanin'." [83]

Giving ourselves, as God did, gives real meaning
to Christmas.

*And whosoever will be chief among you, let him be your
servant: Even as the Son of man came not to be ministered
unto, but to minister, and to give his life a ranson for many.*
MATTHEW 20:27–28

HAPPINESS

Lane was in a state of torment. He had spent a miserable evening pacing the floor. Finally he went to bed, but his troubled mind would not let him sleep. It would not be long until it was time for him to return to Willie's ranch. Once back West, he would be miles and miles away from Ellie. How could he stand never to see her again? If only he had never met her, then he would not know how much he had missed—how much he loved her. She was the kind of woman he had always dreamed of sharing his life with. Her gentle spirit, the sparkle in her eye, her understanding . . .

He had felt that they were so right for each other, and he had been foolish enough to hope and dream that she felt that way, too. *She does, I'm sure she does,* Lane argued with himself. *I'm sure thet she could love me if only*—There it was again. The situation did not change in spite of Lane's yearning. It would be unfair to even ask Ellie to go West if it would bring such pain to Marty. It would be wrong. Ellie, being so sensitive, could not know true happiness if her mother was suffering. It was unthinkable. Even Lane, with his aching heart, knew that.   [118–119]

We cannot expect always to have happiness, for
what brings happiness to one may produce
heartache for another.
*Shall we receive good at the hand of God, and shall we not
receive evil?*
JOB 2:10

145

Mama, do you think Ellie an' Lane had a sweethearts' quarrel?" Kate asked.

"Land sakes," said Marty in bewilderment, "they ain't sweethearts. They're more like brother an' sister."

"Did you ever say that to Ellie?"

"Well, somethin' like thet, maybe."

"An' what did Ellie say?"

"She said thet she didn't want Lane fer a brother," Marty replied, then hesitated. "Now, why would she say a thing like thet?"

"It sounds to me like Lane an' Ellie had 'em a fight."

"I never had me any idea thet they might have thet kind of interest in one another." Marty thought about a number of things that had puzzled her. Kate was right. Things were beginning to *fit*. "When I think on it," Marty said slowly, "they would be well suited to one another. Lane's the most sensitive, carin' young man thet I have ever met. I'm afraid thet I'm already seein' Lane as one of my own. I wonder what happened."

"Sometimes it's the most difficult to understand those closest to us," Kate said, and Marty knew she was right.   [123–124]

The closer we are to something, the less we see of
it. Only from God's perspective is everything seen.
For now we see through a glass, darkly; but then face to face:
now I know in part; but then shall I know even as I am known.
1 CORINTHIANS 13:12

RAPPORT

Marty's needles clicked slowly, revealing that her mind was not on her work.

"What do ya think thet we should do about Ellie and Lane?" she asked Clark.

"Wish I knew fer sure. I'm a-thinkin' thet the only way might jest be to come right straight out with it."

"I think yer right," agreed Marty.

Clark laid his book aside and stood up. "Guess I'll take me a little walk and see what I can find out," he said. Clark walked to the kitchen and bundled up against the cold. He did not hurry. He needed time to think. He needed time to pray. He had no idea how to approach the delicate subject with his daughter. It helped that they had always been able to talk easily to one another. At times like this, Clark was so glad that there had been years of establishing rapport with each of his children. It was well worth it for a father to take the time. [130–131]

Building rapport is like learning First Aid; it seems
unnecessary until someone you love is dying.

Do good, . . . be . . . ready to distribute, willing to communicate;
Laying up in store . . . a good foundation against the
time to come.
1 TIMOTHY 6:18–19

BURDEN-BEARING

Clare took Doc's coat and gave him a report. Marty remained in Kate's room until the doctor appeared; then she busied herself in the kitchen. She didn't know if anyone would want coffee, but making it gave her something to do. With Kate now in the doctor's hands, Marty had time to think. *Would Kate's baby be developed enough to survive? What would happen to Clare and Kate if they lost their baby? What would happen to their faith?*

Marty laid a hand on her own stomach. Her baby responded with a strong kick. "Please, God," Marty prayed, "don't let anythin' happen to the baby. They could never stand it, Lord. They've been workin' an' dreamin' an' prayin' fer thet little 'un fer so long. It would break their hearts to lose it now. Iffen it has to be one of 'em, Lord, then—then take mine. I think thet I could bear it better'n Kate." Even as she spoke her mind filled with the knowledge of the great pain that losing her baby would bring her. If only there was some way to protect Clare and Kate from the awful pain of losing the baby they loved.   [139]

Sometimes it is easier to bear pain ourselves than
to watch someone we love suffer.
O my son Absalom, . . . would God I had died for thee!
2 SAMUEL 18:33

FAIRNESS

Lane came as soon as he heard the news. He spent time with Clare, allowing him to talk out his feelings concerning the death of his infant daughter. It did not seem like the proper time to talk of his intentions to Ellie, so he left his own feelings unspoken. Ellie hardly knew how to respond to Lane, now that she had talked with her ma and pa. They had assured her she was free to make her own future. She hoped her pa was right about Lane not givin' up easily. Ellie feared that Lane might have taken her previous word as the final answer. What if he did not pursue it further? Yet could she be bold enough to approach Lane herself? It wasn't at all in keeping with how she had been brought up, and Ellie doubted very much if she could bring herself to do it.

Marty too had some very difficult days. Each time her child moved, she remembered that she had fought against this baby. She had not wanted it. But Marty loved this baby now. The child within her had completely captured her mother love. Still—she felt guilty. She hadn't wanted it—and yet it was still safe, while Kate and Clare's small baby, which they had wanted so very much, lay in the churchyard under a heap of winter snow. It didn't seem just or fair. [143]

Only God, who sees from beginning to end, can determine what is fair.
Shall mortal man be more just than God?
JOB 4:17

Nandry chatted until Marty poured the coffee and settled down at the table with her. Then she abruptly changed the subject. "Is Kate able to accept it?" she asked.

"Accept it?" said Marty. "Well, it happened, didn't it? One has to accept it—iffen ya want to or not."

"But does Kate feel that God has a right—thet He was fair to do what He done? God could have saved thet baby iffen He had wanted to—jest like He could have saved Pa's leg iffen He had put himself out some. It's true," continued Nandry. "Someone might as well say it. No use jest pretendin' thet it ain't."

Marty laid her hand on Nandry's arm. "It ain't like thet," she began. "God didn't jest take Pa's leg to be spiteful. God done His will an' good came of the sorrow."

"Enough good to make up fer a good man losin' his leg?"

"I think so—" began Marty hesitantly. "The most important was what happened in the life of yer own pa—"

"An' what did *he* ever do to deserve the mercy of God?"

Marty was dumbstruck. What could she ever say to Nandry to help her see that God gives love freely whether a person *deserves* it or not? [145–146]

We can be grateful that God's mercy is not
determined by our merit.
Not by works of righteousness which we have done, but
according to his mercy he saved us.
TITUS 3:5

PERFECTION

Ellie took a deep breath and moved into the room. "Nandry, I think thet I know how yer feelin'. When I heard 'bout Pa, I wanted to fight it too. I blamed God fer spoilin' a good man. I thought thet I might not be proud to walk down the street with Pa anymore. Can you 'magine that? I always thought my pa 'bout perfect, an' I was 'fraid thet I wouldn't see 'im as perfect anymore. It would be embarrassin'. People would stare. I looked at the other men around. 'He's not as good as my pa,' I'd think, 'an' he's still got two legs.' I knew all the time thet it was wrong—an' then God started talkin' to me 'bout it. He pointed at my own life. I had pride, I had vanity; I even discovered some deceit. 'See,' said God, 'yer not perfect. Is yer pa ashamed to walk down the street with you? He should be, iffen it's perfection yer wantin'.' I knew thet God was right. My cripplin' was greater than Pa's. Mine was to the spirit; his was only the body. I asked God to fergive me an' to help me to grow from the experience of Pa losin' his leg, so thet the price of it might be worth somethin' in my life—both fer my gain an' so thet Pa could remain proud of me.

"Pa didn't knowingly give his leg fer yer pa. But I think he would have—iffen he had had some way of knowin'. Because our pa knows thet a leg is less important than a soul." [147–148]

> When our idea of perfection comes from God, we
> don't pay much attention to appearance.
> *Be ye therefore perfect, even as your Father which is in heaven*
> *is perfect.*
> MATTHEW 5:48

BITTERNESS

Wile Ellie spoke Marty prayed that God would give her words that Nandry would understand and accept.

"I think thet Pa would be hurt iffen he knew thet the loss of his leg somehow brought bitterness to yer soul, Nandry. He wants to strengthen ya an' help ya to grow with every experience of his life; and, iffen he doesn't do thet, then it brings him pain and disappointment—far more pain than the loss of thet leg did."

Nandry began to weep. Ellie put her arms about her and let her cry. "Yer right," she said at last. "An' I've been wrong. All these years I've been wrong. My pa wasn't right in what he did, but that gave me no call to do wrong too. I'm more guilty than 'im all those years. 'Let 'im git what he deserves,' I'd think. Thet was wrong—so wrong. Oh, Ellie, can God ever fergive me?"

"Iffen He couldn't," said Ellie, "we'd all be in trouble."

"Ma," wept Nandry, seeming to suddenly realize that Marty still sat nearby, "would ya pray fer me?"

Marty did. Ellie followed in prayer, and then Nandry cried out her own pleading to God. [148]

We don't realize how bitterness weighs us down
until we give it up.
Follow peace with all men, and holiness, . . . lest any root of
bitterness springing up trouble you, and thereby
many be defiled.
HEBREWS 12:14 –15

TRUST

After the prayer time, Marty stayed at the table rejoicing and doing some serious thinking. Nandry had been wrong to bundle up all of her years of bitterness. She should have been able to trust God. She had been taught ever since she had come to live in the Davis home that God is *God* in all circumstances of our lives, and He loves His children. Nothing happens to those He loves that catches Him by surprise. He is always there to see us through the difficulty and to bear us up on wings of love. God *can* follow on the path of sorrow. All things *can* work for good to those who love Him.

Marty knew it all. She even believed it all. So why was she sitting at her kitchen table when just across the yard was her daughter-in-law who needed her? *I don't know what to say,* pleaded Marty. *I still have my baby. An', God, Ya know thet I want my baby. Is thet selfish? Can I go to Kate, with me so obviously expectin' my child, when she has jest lost hers?*

Trust Me came a quiet voice. Marty wiped her eyes on her apron and rose from her chair. She would take Kate the new shawl that she had been knitting. Perhaps she would welcome something new and bright on this dreary winter day. [149]

How can we say we trust God if we're afraid to
obey Him?
Trust in the LORD, and do good.
PSALM 37:3

BLESSINGS

Kate blinked back tears. "I'm sorry too, Mama. But Doc said thet God sometimes uses thet way to care fer a baby thet has some kind of problem. I thought of Wanda, Mama. I know thet Wanda loves her Rett and thet she wouldn't give him up fer the world, but I'm not sure thet I could take thet, Mama. Am I a coward to feel thet way?"

"A coward? No, Kate. Certainly not. I think thet there are harder things to face in life than death."

"Clare an' I talked 'bout it. It was so hard. We wanted our baby so much, an' then Clare said, 'Let's jest count the blessin's outa all this.' At first I couldn't see 'em. Clare had to remind me. 'We don't have a child who is sickly, either in mind or in body. She will never suffer. She is safe in heaven, without even sufferin' any of the pains of this earth. An' we still have each other an' can have more babies.' So, ya see, we do have lots to be thankful fer. We've grown through this, Mama. We're grown closer together. I've always loved Clare, but now I not only love 'im, I respect 'im as the spiritual leader of our home."

Marty took the younger woman's hand. She had come to minister to Kate, but instead Kate was ministering to her.   [151–152]

Buried under the biggest burden is a good place to
find an even bigger blessing.
*Sorrow is better than laughter: for by the sadness of the
countenance the heart is made better.*
ECCLESIASTES 7:3

You'll never know jest how set I was on feelin' sorry fer myself before Christmas," Ma explained. "I didn't really tell ya all thet I was feelin', but I was all set fer a good, long bitter spell. I felt thet it jest wasn't fair thet I should lose two good men in a lifetime. Some women don't even like the one they got, I reasoned, an' here I was with two thet I had loved deeply an' I lost 'em both. Didn't seem fair somehow. Didn't even seem worth fightin' to keep up a good front fer the kids. Then ya came by an' made me realize thet it did still matter to my kids. I started thinkin' on it an' I saw somethin' else too. True, some women don't like the man they got. Thet's to their sorrow. I had me two good companions. Now, how many women could be so lucky? An' here I was a-fussin' 'bout it."

Marty smiled at Ma's reasoning.

"So I decided," continued Ma, "thet I jest should be thankin' the Lord fer all the good years 'stead of fussin' 'bout the years to come."

"An' it helped?"

"Ya bet it helped. Every day I think of somethin' more to be thankful fer. I have a good family—mine an' Ben's. That's truly somethin' to be thankful fer."   [165–166]

> Instead of crying over what has been taken *from*
> us, we should consider what has been given *to* us.
> *In everything give thanks: for this is the will of God in Christ*
> *Jesus concerning you.*
> 1 THESSALONIANS 5:18

WORDS & ACTIONS

The wedding dinner was a festive affair. Family and neighbors laughed and chatted and ate until they could eat no more. Ellie exclaimed over every gift with a great deal of enthusiasm, and Lane gave a little speech.

"I will ever bless the day when my boss had the good sense to order me on east to care fer a farm," Lane said amid laughter. "Tell the truth, I wasn't lookin' forward much to bein' a farmer—never havin' been one. Iffen I hadn't met Ma and Pa Davis an' looked forward to seein' 'em again, I don't s'pose thet even the boss coulda made a farmer outa me. Boy, what I woulda missed!" exclaimed Lane, his eyes full of Ellie.

Lane became more serious then. "I've got lots to learn yet in life. Lots to learn in the Christian walk, but I've already learned this. Iffen I let God control things, He can do a heap better job of it than I ever could. I jest have no way of sayin' how thankful I am fer a girl like Ellie—how lucky I am to have her fer a wife. I can't express it no-how—but I hope to spend my lifetime a-tryin' to show her how I feel." [198–199]

What a few words can't say, a lifetime of action can.

Let us not love in word, neither in tongue; but in deed and in truth.
1 JOHN 3:18

LEGACIES

Baby Belinda lay between Clark and Marty. She studied their faces as they bent over her. With one of her hands clasped firmly to her father's finger and the other tiny fist knotted in the front of Marty's gown, she held them both. Not just with childish fingers but with cords of love.

"I been thinkin' a lot on legacies lately," Clark said, brushing one of Belinda's curls. "I'm not talkin' money in the bank. I'm talkin' character—faith . . . love fer others . . . an unselfish spirit . . . independence . . . maturity. We've got a big job ahead of us, Marty. It'll be fun—but there will be work, too."

"I was thinkin' the other day," admitted Marty, 'here I go again! The diapers, the fevers, the teeth, the potty-trainin'.' Oh, Clark. There's so much ahead of us."

"Wish it was as simple as passin' on family heirlooms. Ya don't jest pass on faith. Ya have to pass on a desire fer 'em to find a faith of their own. Ya have to show 'em daily in the way thet ya live thet what ya have is worth livin' fer. A second-hand faith is no good to anyone. An' it doesn't stop there—it goes on an' on. They teach an' train our grandchildren, an' with God's help, they teach our great-grandchildren. It can go on an' on, an' never end 'til Jesus comes back. It's a legacy thet truly lasts." [221–224]

What we invest in lives has lasting value.
And these words . . . shall be in thine heart: and thou shalt
teach them diligently unto thy children.
DEUTERONOMY 6:6–7

LOVE'S UNFOLDING

DREAM

SAVING LIFE

Look!" Belinda cried in a choking voice. In her outstretched hand lay a small sparrow, its feathers ruffled and wet, its head dipping awkwardly to the side. "The mother cat had it!" Belinda wailed. I had to chase her all over the barn!" The small girl buried her head against Marty. "It's gonna die, isn't it?"

"Well, I—I don't know," stammered Marty, taking another look at the injured bird. Yes, barring a miracle it would die. But it was difficult for her to say those words to Belinda. *Oh, God,* she prayed silently, *I know it's jest a sparrow, but Ya said that Ya see each sparrow thet falls. If Yer heart is as heavy as Belinda's over this one, then could Ya please make it well again?*

As Marty finished taking the biscuits from the pan, Belinda gave a little cry. "I think it's already dead," she said in a sobbing whisper. "Look! It's gittin' stiff."

Belinda was right. The sparrow was already past the help of even Doctor Luke. Marty put her arms around her daughter to comfort her. Belinda was so much like her big brother Luke. *Life is going to be so painful for Belinda,* Marty lamented. How many hurts—deep hurts—lay down the road for their youngest child? She trembled at the thought. [13–20]

Doctors can postpone death, but only God can overcome it.
He that heareth my word, and believeth on him that sent me, hath everlasting life.
JOHN 5:24

A SPECIAL PLACE

Belinda made a small box for the sparrow to be buried in, called on her cousin Amy Jo and the three boys to join her in a ceremony after supper, and wept as the small bird joined a number of other small graves at the far end of the garden. When it was over the girl's thoughts returned to childhood play.

Belinda was usually a happy, well-adjusted child. *If only she did not grieve so when she found little creatures dead or dying,* Marty wished. She hoped the young girl eventually would learn to face the realities of life with a bit less emotional turmoil. No one liked suffering. But some pain was inevitable.

Clark came toward the house, carrying a pail brimming with white foaming milk. "She looks fine now," he stated, nodding his head in Belinda's direction.

"Oh, she usually snaps back—but, my, what a storm of tears in the meantime," responded Marty.

"Guess I'd rather have her on the tender side than calloused an' uncarin'," Clark commented. "Jest pray thet all thet compassion gits put to proper use. God must have Him a special place fer someone like our Belinda." [22–23]

God gives every believer a special gift and a
special place to use it.
*We, being many, are one body in Christ, and every one
members one of another. Having . . . gifts differing according to
the grace that is given to us.*
ROMANS 12:5–6

EXPRESSING CONCERN

Soaking off the bloody bandages was a slow process. At least it seemed awfully slow to Belinda on this first opportunity to assist her brother on one of his house calls. She marveled at Luke's patience. At last the final bit of gauze was lifted from the cut, and Belinda caught her breath as she saw the angry red tear in the flesh. It had been stitched carefully so there was no gaping, but it was still inflamed and fiery looking. Belinda lifted her eyes back to the face of the patient. *It must be very painful. How did Sam——?*

There was pain in Sam's eyes. Without even thinking, Belinda reached out a hand and brushed the shaggy hair back from his forehead. For just a second their eyes met. A message of sympathy passed from Belinda to Sam, and then the spell was broken. Quickly Belinda withdrew her hand and stepped back, and Sam restlessly moved his head on the pillow.

Luke saw it all—the compassion that prompted Belinda's action, the brief moment of accepted sympathy on the part of Sam, and the hasty retreat by both of them. *Why do we do it?* Luke wondered. *Why do we feel we can't honestly, openly express our concern for another?* [43–44]

When our concern is genuine, the fear of being misunderstood shouldn't keep us from expressing it.

Be ye all of one mind, having compassion one of another.
1 PETER 3:8

CHILDREN AS PEOPLE

Over coffee at Kate's, Marty discussed the idea of redoing Amy Jo's room as her birthday present. Kate was thrilled.

"I should have thought to let her do her own choosin' before," said Kate.

"I saw, firsthand, some of Amy Jo's choices," Marty replied. "Ya better be preparin' yerself is all thet I can say. I hope thet ya like yer rooms colorful an' bright."

Kate laughed. "I've seen a few of her choices. They are a bit shockin', aren't they? Well, I guess we will jest learn to live with 'em. I'm realizin' more an' more thet it's like you an' Pa have often said. They grow up awful fast, an' soon they won't be with us at all." Kate poured more coffee, then went on reflectively, "Besides feedin' and clothin' and trainin' our children, Clare an' I need to be listenin' to 'em an' learnin' to know 'em as people on their own whilst we've still got the chance."   [58–59]

When we pay attention to our children's strengths
and weaknesses, we are better able to "train them
in the way they should go."
Train up a child in the way he should go: and when he is old,
he will not depart from it.
PROVERBS 22:6

EXPECTATIONS

Marty found the children just as Kate had said—sprawled on the bed or on rugs and pillows across the floor of Belinda's room, all eyes fixed on Melissa. No one even stirred as Marty peeked around the door. *Well, I declare*, she said to herself. *Iffen thet don't beat all.* She went back down the stairs to assure the rest that Kate had not been fooling. "Never seed nothin' like it. Every last one of 'em. Quiet as you please."

"It sure is nice to have Melissa here," Marty said softly. "She's the sweetest thing ya ever saw."

Clare nodded in agreement. "She's sweet, thet's fer sure— but let's not put the burden of perfection on 'er. She's human after all, Ma. Let's leave her some room to make some mistakes— have some flaws. She's gonna find plenty of 'em in us. Reckon we ought to allow her a few as well."

Clare was right. Melissa was bound to have *some* weaknesses. They just hadn't seen them yet. Well, whatever they were, Marty would still love her, she decided. But even as Marty assured herself of that, she couldn't imagine anything that could possibly be wrong with Missie's little girl. [87–88]

Unrealistic expectations may lead to unexpected disappointment.

And [Jesus] cometh, and findeth them sleeping, and saith unto Peter, Simon, sleepest thou? Couldest not thou watch one hour?

MARK 14:37

EMOTIONAL HEALING

After the emergency surgery Belinda took a good look at the patient for the first time. He was young, no more than seventeen or eighteen, she guessed. And he was deathly pale. She wondered how he would feel when he wakened. There would still be pain, Belinda knew. He would be in pain for many days—weeks, even. But he would not have an arm. What a terrible thing to happen to a young man.

Belinda thought of her pa and his missing leg. It had been hard for him, she knew that. But he had been a grown man. And he had had the Lord to help him. Faith in his heavenly Father had gotten him through. What about the young man before her? Did he know the Lord? Belinda feared not. Without taking her eyes from the pale face before her, Belinda began to pray, her voice no more than a whisper.

"Oh, God," she implored, "I don't know this boy. I don't know iffen he knows You, but he's gonna need Ya, God. He's gonna need Ya to help him accept this awful thing thet has happened in his life. He's gonna need Ya to help him git better agin." Without thinking Belinda brushed the hair back from his pale, sweat-dampened forehead. [112–113]

> With some injuries, the body heals faster than
> the emotions.
> *He healeth the broken in heart, and bindeth up their wounds.*
> PSALM 147:3

BOREDOM

Marty didn't want to appear as if she were hanging around to see if Mrs. Simpson knew what she was doing, but she had nothing to take her attention. She went upstairs and wandered aimlessly for a few minutes, fluffing pillows and arranging curtains; then she sat down on the side of her bed. *This is silly*, she told herself. *Here I am, 'most a prisoner in my own home. How am I ever gonna make it through the next few days? How many days is Clark hirin' 'em, anyway? An' what am I gonna do with my time?*

A little voice within her responded. *You could pray. You are always saying that you wish you had more praying time.*

Marty knelt beside her bed. Before long she found herself truly communicating with God—talking to Him from her heart and hearing His responses the same way. She remembered the special needs of every one of her family members. She prayed for the neighbors, for the church, and for the new schoolteacher. Then she prayed for the Simpson family and for their son's adjustment to the loss of his arm.

Marty returned to her kitchen refreshed, and surprised at how much time had passed. It had been a long, long time since she'd had so much of her morning to spend in prayer.   [158–161]

When we feel as if we have nothing to do, perhaps
God is giving us time to pray.
The effectual fervent prayer of a righteous man availeth much.
JAMES 5:16

WELCOME

I've enjoyed havin' ya here," Marty said to Mrs. Simpson. "It's been nice workin' with ya. An' we'd be so happy iffen ya'd join us in worship at our church. It's not fancy like, but you an' yer family would be most welcome—"

She was cut short. Mrs. Simpson's eyes sparked as she flung a hand toward her tattered dress. "Like this?" she hissed. "I'm not thinkin' that much of a welcome mat would be extended to people lookin' like this."

Before Marty could respond, the woman grabbed her coat from the peg, pushed her way out the door, and was gone.

Marty looked after her in stunned silence. *Oh, God,* she prayed, *forgive us iffen we have given thet impression. Why would she think thet we wouldn't welcome her the way thet she be? I so much wanted her to know thet she was welcome into my house an' she'd be welcome into Yer house, too, but somehow I have failed Ya agin, Lord.* Then, from somewhere within Marty came a reply. *Be patient,* the gentle voice said. *Just be patient. I have never failed you, and I am with the Simpsons, too, even when they are not aware of it.* [165]

If we don't make poor people feel welcome, maybe
our standards are different from God's.

The LORD will maintain the cause of the afflicted, and the right

of the poor.
PSALM 140:12

Luke bathed the child's teary face with a warm cloth and smoothed back her tangled hair.

"How—how many more times do we need to go through this?" the young mother asked, her eyes filled with agony.

"I really can't say," Luke said. "It's going to be a fight to keep out infection. We'll have to keep a close watch on it. But once it starts to heal properly, it might improve quite quickly. With a child, it often does," he assured her, patting the child's head. Luke smiled at the woman. "We'll do the best we can," he promised. Luke gathered all his belongings and reached for his coat. Outside, he laid his hand on Belinda's shoulder. "Thanks," he said. "I never could have done it without you. Do you mind coming back a few times to give me a hand?"

"No—I don't mind. I'll help."

"It's not very nice, is it?"

"No," admitted Belinda.

"It's always harder when it's a child," said Luke, shaking his head. "The poor little things just can't understand the pain—and the treatment." [183–184]

When it comes to spiritual healing, adults often
misunderstand the pain of God's treatment.

Think it not strange concerning the fiery trial which is to try
you. . . . But rejoice, inasmuch as ye are partakers of
Christ's suffering.
1 PETER 4:12–13

CHARITY

Over the weeks Marty watched Mrs. Simpson's eyes go from despair, to acceptance, to hope, to renewed faith in life. The family was still in difficult financial circumstances, but they were on their way to independence. Mrs. Simpson wore a new dress, one she had made for herself with money she earned from sewing jobs Marty got for her. She even walked with more confidence now that she was no longer wearing the oft-mended garment.

Marty learned that Mrs. Simpson's two sons had never been to school, even though both parents put great stock in education and had taught the boys everything they could, bringing home extra books to help them keep up with other youngsters their age. Mr. Simpson was a college graduate, and Mrs. Simpson had tutored special English classes to immigrant families. Marty understood a bit more about the pride that kept them from "accepting charity." [197]

We need not be any more reluctant to accept
charity when we need it than we are to give it
when others need it.

*And all that believed were together, and had all things
common; and sold their possessions and goods, and parted
them to all men, as every man had need.*

ACTS 2:44–45

WANTING MORE

Belinda frequently wondered about Drew Simpson. Was he still nursing his grief? Although Belinda saw Mrs. Simpson often, she did not ask about Drew. Not that she did not care. It was just that she feared the answer might not be the one she wanted to hear.

Jackson still hung around—*a hard one to avoid*, Belinda decided. Even though school was out for the summer, Belinda saw him each Sunday at church and he always lingered, looking for some opportunity to serve her or suggesting some outing they might enjoy together. Belinda tried to be kind and firm, but Jackson was not too good at taking hints.

Melissa sighed and longed for Jackson to notice her. Other boys would have gladly showered Melissa with their attention, but she ignored them completely.

How foolish we be, thought Marty as she watched silently from the sidelines. *Each wantin' exactly what one can't have.*   [197–198]

> If we'd spend more time taking care of what we
> have and less time wanting what we don't have,
> we might find out that we already have
> what we want.
>
> *O fear the LORD, ye his saints: for there is no want to them
> that fear him. . . . They that seek the LORD shall not want any
> good thing.*
> PSALM 34:9–10

INNER STRUGGLE

All through the spring and summer Drew struggled with his bitterness. Why had he lost his arm? If God cared about him, why did He allow it to happen? Why hadn't the doctor just let him die? He would rather be dead. At least he *thought* he'd rather be dead. He seemed to be at war with himself. Part of him kept fighting to be free of the bitterness. At other times he wanted to give in to his bitter feelings, but something unseen kept him from doing it.

How was Drew to know that he was the subject of daily prayers? How was he to understand that the strange longing, the reaching for something beyond himself, was the result of God's working in answer to the prayers of people who cared?

But just as he felt ready to let his anger go, his stump of an arm would catch his attention and a new wave of pain would sear through him. Sobs of pain and anguish would cause Drew to bury his head in his pillow or flee the house in renewed bitterness.

And so Drew struggled with himself. One minute he was content to wrap himself securely in his shell of bitterness and pain, and the next minute almost responding to the urge within himself to let go of his bitterness—to try to find some other way to live with what "fate" had handed him. [206–207]

When we're fighting an inner battle, we need
strength from an outer source.
My strength is made perfect in weakness.
2 CORINTHIANS 12:9

LOSING BITTERNESS

Drew did not understand the Davis family, but he could sense that they were different. He had never seen a woman as sensitive—as caring—as Mrs. Davis. And the father. The man with just one leg. Why did he have such a warm and generous spirit? The whole thing was beyond Drew—until one day when Clark had a chance to explain.

"At first I thought my whole world had fallen apart. I wondered how I would care fer my family. Fer a little while I wished thet I had died. But soon God reminded me thet I had a lot to live fer. Thet my family loved me and would keep right on lovin' me—one leg or two—an' thet God hadn't forgotten me. It took a while, but God helped me to accept it." Clark stopped. The boy who had been discussing the loss of a limb so calmly suddenly started sobbing convulsively.

"I hate it!" he screamed. "I don't have an arm. I don't have a God. I don't have nothin'."

Clark held him until he quieted. Then he said, "Son, I can't do nothin' 'bout gittin' ya an arm, but I do know where ya can find yerself a God."

And so it was that Drew found his God and lost his bitterness.

[209–214]

It is impossible to lose our bitterness without
finding God first.
*I love them that love me; and those that seek me early
shall find me.*
PROVERBS 8:17

CONFIDENCE

I don't know how it works," Drew began, "but it does. Somehow God really does change you when you ask Him to."

"I know," smiled Belinda. "He changed me, too. And I've been prayin' for you. Ever since your accident."

"What did you ask?" Drew wanted to know.

"Thet you'd get better. Thet you wouldn't be bitter."

"Bet you thought God hadn't heard your prayer, huh?

"Sometimes it takes a while. We need to learn patience when prayin'. Pa is always sayin' thet."

"What ya gonna do after your last year of school?"

"Luke's gonna let me work in his office. He'll train me and I'll help him there an' with his house calls."

"I wanted to get some trainin', too," Drew said after a long silence. "I always wanted to be a lawyer. It woulda been tough enough when I had both arms, but now, I'd never be able to—"

"Thet makes no diffcrence," Belinda boldly interrupted. "Ya don't need two hands to think, an' lawyers mostly think, an' talk. Ya can still do thet. Ya got a good head. No reason ya can't still be a lawyer iffen ya want to."

"You really think I could?" Drew wanted to hug her for giving him back his dream. [218–221]

Confidence in ourselves begins with confidence in God.
This is the confidence that we have in him, that, if we ask any thing according to his will, he heareth us.
1 JOHN 5:14 –15

LOVE TAKES

WING

THE SPEED OF LIFE

Amy Jo went wild with excitement when she learned she could travel west with her cousin Melissa. Both girls begged Belinda to join them, but Belinda answered firmly that she was needed in Luke's office.

Bags, trunks and boxes were packed in a flurry of excitement. All too soon for those left standing on the wooden platform, the west-bound train chugged off, its whistle sounding shrilly in the afternoon air.

Belinda looked about at her world. Why did things have to keep changing? Spring, without slowing down even for a minute, turned to summer and summer to fall. One hardly had time to turn around and things were all new and different again.

Things had seemed so simple, so secure when Belinda had been a child going to school and sharing girlish games with Amy Jo, her constant companion. But life went on and no amount of "digging in one's heels" seemed to slow it down.   [42–43, 73–74]

When we are five, a year is one-fifth of our life;
when we are sixty, it's one-sixtieth. Time seems to
go faster the older we get because each additional
year is a smaller percentage of the total time we
have lived.

I have been young, and now am old; yet have I not seen the
righteous forsaken.
PSALM 37:25

THE PAIN OF FIXING

Arnie swung around to face Luke, his eyes black with anger. "Are ya suggestin' thet I take my son to some city hospital and put 'im through his pain all over again—on purpose? Well, forget it," rasped out Arnie. "The boy has suffered enough. Iffen you'd set it properlike in the first place—"

"Arnie," said Luke gently, "I don't blame you for feeling that way. Honest, I don't. And I wouldn't even suggest such a thing if there was any other way. But I've been watching that arm. It's getting worse. It needs to be fixed and the sooner the better."

"I said no." Arnie's voice was low but the tone unmistakable. "I won't put him through all thet. He's been through enough pain already," he insisted. "What kind of pa would I be to put him through more?"

"A loving pa," Luke said, laying a hand on Arnie's arm, his voice little more than a whisper.

Arnie spun around to face him. "You doctors!" he cried, choking on his words, "all ya wanna do is play God. Ya don't think anythin' 'bout the pain ya cause." [85]

> Fixing sin is painful temporarily; not fixing sin is
> painful eternally.
> *No chastening for the present seemeth to be joyous, but*
> *grievous: nevertheless afterward it yieldeth the peaceable fruit*
> *of righteousness unto them which are exercised thereby.*
> HEBREWS 12:11

FLESH & BLOOD

Belinda couldn't believe that her own brother—tender, sensitive Arnie—could say such cruel things to Luke. He had always been so loving—so caring. *Arnie must be deeply hurt to have changed so much—so completely,* she reasoned.

"I've never felt so heavy-hearted in all my life," admitted Marty. "To see those I love so much hurtin' and not speakin' is jest 'most more'n I can bear. And I never saw yer pa suffer so. Even his leg didn't lay 'im as low as this has. His leg was jest—jest flesh an' bone—but this—this is—is flesh an' *blood*." Marty shook her head slowly. "Maybe we been takin' the family fer granted," she said. "When ya have it all together, lovin' an' supportin' one another, ya don't realize how blessed ya are. Iffen ya got yer family—then ya have most of what ya really need."   [95–96]

When there's division in God's family, the whole family suffers.

I beseech you, brethren, by the name of our Lord Jesus Christ, that ye all speak the same thing, and that there be no divisions among you; but that ye be perfectly joined together in the same mind and in the same judgment.

1 CORINTHIANS 1:10

TAKING ACTION

Marty finally decided to take matters into her own hands. She bundled herself up and set out for Arnie's. Arnie sat down at the table with her, and Marty reached out a hand and laid it on his. "Arnie," she said, "you have always been the tenderest member of the family—have felt things the deepest—an' said the least. I know how the hurtin' of young Abe has brought ya deep pain. We have all suffered—we love the boy—but you have suffered the most."

Marty paused. Arnie's eyes were fastened on his cup, but he had not withdrawn his hand. Marty took courage and went on. "We miss ya, Arnie—you an' the kids—an' Anne. We need ya—as a family we need ya. The family isn't—isn't whole anymore. We all feel it. It hurts. Real bad. It's not as God intended it to be. Would ya come back, Arnie?" Marty pleaded. "Would ya come back to yer family? To yer church? We love ya, Arnie. We need ya. Please. Please come home."

Arnie's face convulsed, and he laid his head on his arms. Marty leaned over to hold her broken son. She soothed and comforted and stroked his hair as she had done when he had been a child. Then she kissed his cheek and slipped into her coat. She had done all she could.

[97–98]

We cannot make people change, but we can make it as easy as possible for them to do so.

If a man be overtaken in a fault . . . restore such an one in the spirit of meekness.

GALATIANS 6:1

TRYING TOO HARD

Arnie did come back. He came to church the next Sunday, though he sat stiffly in the pew. The children were thrilled to be back, and Marty noticed a more peaceful look in Anne's eyes.

Arnie also joined the family at Clare's house for dinner. Everyone was very cautious about the words they spoke—so much so that the conversation often lagged. At times the tension in the air was so heavy that one felt choked by it.

The family was back together—at least bodily. But it wasn't the same, not the same at all. They all tried so hard—too hard—to make things as they had always been. The chatter, the teasing, the concerns over one another's affairs—all meant to bring back the feeling of family—all failed miserably. The unity had been broken. The bond had been weakened. They were not as they had been.

Marty talked to Clark about it on the short walk home. She longed for the old relationship to be restored, but she was at a loss as to how it could be done. She didn't have any answers and there seemed to be so many troubling questions. [98–99]

Getting people inside the same house doesn't
mean there is unity.

How good and how pleasant it is for brethren to dwell together

in unity.

PSALM 133:1

STRAINED RELATIONSHIP

Belinda turned a concerned face to her mother, then reached out a comforting hand and touched her cheek.

"Luke an' I are both prayin'—"she told Marty, "prayin' thet those special meetin's might turn things right around. God can, you know. Arnie can still—"

"It's more than jest young Abe," Marty interrupted. "It's beyond thet now. Sometimes I look at Arnie an' I see such pain in his eyes thet I can scarcely stand it. I think thet he is hurtin' far more than thet boy. He still comes to church, but he doesn't take part in anythin'. Jest sits. I sometimes wonder iffen he's even listenin'. I'm guessin' he's still angry with Luke an' Clare—an'—maybe even with God."

The country church meetings with the special speaker began. Arnie went to the first meeting and then declared himself too busy to go back on successive nights. But Luke went. Every night he could possibly get away. He had been feelin' a "dryness"—a need for spiritual refreshing. The strained relationship with Arnie had cut him deeply. He knew that only God could meet his inner need and, ultimately, mend the broken family relationships.

[137–138]

Human effort can bring people together physically,
but only God's effort can bring them together spiritually.
*If we walk in the light, as he is in the light, we have fellowship
one with another.*
1 JOHN 1:7

A WEIGHT LIFTED

Marty knew the moment she looked at Luke's face that something important had happened. "Ya look like a heavy weight's been lifted off yer shoulders," she observed.

Luke smiled. "Not my shoulders—my heart," he said. "Those meetings were just what I needed to get things back into proper focus. I'm on my way over to see Arnie."

"To tell 'em ya forgive him?" Marty asked eagerly.

Luke looked surprised. "No, I am going to beg my brother to forgive me," said Luke soberly.

"But Arnie was angry with you," Marty said.

"And for good reason," Luke explained. "I had no business butting into his life, assuming that I knew what was best for his son, demanding that he see things my way. I didn't mean to be arrogant and self-righteous, but I was. I just hope and pray that Arnie can find it in his heart to forgive me."

Marty took Luke's hand. "Yer pa an' me'll be prayin' the whole time it takes ya to talk to Arnie."

"I think we should start now," Clark stated, and he bowed his head and led the little group in prayer. [145–146]

A heavy heart weighs more than any other burden.
First, cast the beam out of thine own eye; and then shalt thou
see clearly to cast the mote out of thy brother's eye.
MATTHEW 7:5

Are ya comfortable?" Belinda asked Mrs. Stafford-Smyth, a woman from Boston whom Belinda had been nursing for several months. After getting her new employer settled, Belinda leaned against the velvet seat of the Pullman. *I'm actually on my way to Boston! And I am not ready to marry either Rand O'Connel or Jackson Brown.* With that settled, she turned her attention back to her patient.

"Stop fussing so," scolded Mrs. Stafford-Smyth good-naturedly. "This is your first trip. Enjoy it."

Belinda moved closer to the window. The landscape soon began to change. The trees were bigger, the forests more dense. *This is a new world for me,* she said to herself. But she didn't realize how different until they arrived at Mrs. Stafford-Smyth's home, which was now her home as well.

"Welcome to Marshall Manor," said Mrs. Stafford-Smyth.

"Oh, my!" was the only response Belinda could manage. The house was nestled on a wide expanse of carefully manicured green lawn with flowerbeds filled with hollyhock, daisies, and begonias. The driveway of red stone circled to the wide front step, and an arched brick canopy reached out to give protection from the weather. Belinda felt as if she had stepped into a fairy tale. The place was absolutely breathtaking. [151–157]

When life seems like a fairy tale, it's time to watch
out for the big bad wolf of temptation.
Watch ye and pray, lest ye enter into temptation.
MARK 14:38

ISOLATED

Belinda had looked forward all week to meeting with God's people on Sunday. But the Boston church was nothing like the little country church at home. Its spires seemed to reach to the clouds, and the building seemed even more massive inside. The people looked small and insignificant. Strains of music from a giant pipe organ rose and fell, wafting her spirit up in lovely ecstasy and then bringing it back down to gentle peace again. Her heart throbbed. How easy it must be to worship God in such a majestic setting! Belinda's heart swelled in praise and gratitude to God for all His goodness.

Belinda was surprised that the people didn't look excited about being in such a glorious place of worship. A cold chill passed through her. She turned her attention to the platform, but the robed men were so far away she couldn't see the expressions on their faces. Their voices sounded like distant echoes. The words were familiar, and they lifted her spirit. But the beautiful, large stone church still seemed cold and distant—the people masked and aloof. There were no welcoming smiles or gentle nods. Belinda wondered what was wrong with her. *They must know—without me even sayin'—thet I come from the plains,* she concluded. And Belinda felt alone and isolated.   [173–174]

Beauty outside is no guarantee of warmth inside.
We have a building of God, an house not made with hands,
eternal in the heavens.
2 CORINTHIANS 5:1

ACCEPTING THE GIFT

Mrs. Stafford-Smyth chuckled. Belinda's fire of enthusiasm seemed to ignite something in her soul. "If it means so much to you, then go ahead. Do whatever you like."

"No! Not me. Us! You need Christmas as much as I do."

Mrs. Stafford-Smyth chuckled again. "Well, if it pleases you— then of course we'll have Christmas."

The next few days were spent in frenzied but joyful activity. A whole new air of excitement pervaded the house that had so long been silent and empty. "I think we need some guests," said Belinda. "I'll see if one of the ministers knows of any new folks in town who are away from their families."

When Christmas Day dawned cold and windy, Belinda wondered if anyone would come. But at ten of five the knocker sounded and Windsor began admitting guests. After the meal, Mrs. Stafford-Smyth distributed a small gift to each one, and all too soon it was time to say farewell. Mrs. Stafford-Smyth and Belinda settled before the crackling fire for a last cup of hot cider.

"Thank you," said the older woman softly. "Thank you for giving me another Christmas."

"Oh, but I didn't give Christmas," Belinda corrected gently. "He did. We just accepted His gift." [206–208]

We have nothing to give others except what God
has given us.

A man can receive nothing, except it be given him from heaven.
JOHN 3:27

DRIFTING FROM GOD

Something in what the kindly man said stirred Belinda. Had she left God in her homeland? Was that why her trip abroad had been so dismal, so unsatisfying? She had missed attending church, but had she misplaced God, too? His true dwelling is in hearts. Had she shut the door of her heart when she stepped on the deck of the sailing vessel? *No!* Belinda realized. She had left God out of her life even before leaving Boston. Perhaps the downward slide had started with her restlessness back in her own small town. She had allowed her nursing duties to keep her from daily times of prayer and Bible reading. *And I was getting all nervous and upset about Rand and Jackson*, she remembered.

Belinda drew her Bible from the bottom of a suitcase and clasped the book to her bosom. "Oh, God," she prayed, "I'm so sorry. Forgive me for forsaking you. I've been so lonely, and in my foolishness I did not even know why." [216–217]

When nothing seems satisfying, we may be
looking for satisfaction in something other than
God.

*As for me, I will behold thy face in righteousness: I shall be
satisfied when I awake with thy likeness.*

PSALM 17:15

SATAN'S SUBTLETY

It was a while before the storm was spent and peace again entered Belinda's heart. She sat on her berth and read favorite portions from her precious book, wondering how she had become so careless as to have neglected it. She knew the importance of Bible reading and prayer. How had she let the pleasures of the world and the deceitfulness of leisure and wealth lead her so far off course? How could Satan so subtly and slowly have drawn her away from her source of spiritual life? *It's not that the Lord doesn't want me to enjoy beautiful things and interesting places*, Belinda decided. *But He wants me to do those things with Him, not without Him.*

Feeling renewed and alive again, Belinda laid her Bible on the bedside table and thought about ways to tell Mrs. Stafford-Smyth about her new discovery. She had not been the Christian witness to the woman that she should have been. She prayed that God would help her to change all that. Knowing that she served a merciful and understanding God, Belinda was confident that she would be given opportunity to share her faith properly in the future. [218]

Satan doesn't always pursue us like a hunter with
a deadly weapon; sometimes he lures us like a
trout fisherman with an irresistible fly.

*But I fear . . . as the serpent beguiled Eve through subtilty, so your
minds should be corrupted from the simplicity that is in Christ.*
2 CORINTHIANS 11:3

LOVE FINDS

A HOME

NAMESAKE

Thomas could not repress his smile or the shine in his eyes. His gnarled old hand reached forward to caress the flower, and before Belinda could catch her breath, he snipped it from the stem and extended it to her. " 'Tis only fitting ye be the one to have the first bloom." He lowered his eyes to his worn-out gardener's shoes. "I named her Belinda," he confessed. "Princess Belinda."

Breathing deeply of the fragrance, Belinda brushed her lips against the soft petals. "It's beautiful," she whispered. "Thank you, Thomas."

As she walked toward the veranda, Belinda studied the flower. The soft cream of each petal blended into a deeper yellow, which then changed to apricot. Belinda had never seen such a pretty rose. *What a difference one bright flower can make in a person's life,* she mused. But then she corrected herself. *No, it isn't the flower— pretty as it is. It is a person who has brought joy to my heart. Thomas. A dear old man—just a gardener in some folks' thinking—but a beautiful person. One I have learned to love."* [18–19]

Unimpressive people can make lasting
impressions with a simple act of kindness.
*But the fruit of the Spirit is love, joy, peace, longsuffering,
gentleness, goodness, faith.*
GALATIANS 5:22

NOSTALGIA

Belinda chose a favorite book and went to the garden swing. She had intended to read, but being home brought back memories of her childhood companions, Amy Jo and Melissa, and she couldn't concentrate. *Why do things have to change?* she asked herself. *Why couldn't we have just stayed in our innocence, our childish bliss?* But even as she asked, she knew the answer. They had longed to become adults, feeling that they were growing up way too slowly. And now they were both hundreds of miles away, with homes of their own.

The nostalgic thoughts drove Belinda from the swing. She wandered to the garden. The goldenrod glowed brightly in the fall sunshine, and the asters lifted proud heads, their colors varied and vibrant. She moved on, admiring the other flowers. *They are pretty,* she mused, *though nothing like Thomas's tailored flower beds. What's the matter with me?* Belinda thought crossly. *When I'm in Boston, I'm longing for the farm; and when I'm on the farm, I'm secretly longing for Boston. Don't I fit in anywhere anymore?*   [68–69]

In a short time, what is happening today will be
the past you fondly remember.
*For I know the thoughts that I think toward you, saith the
LORD, thoughts of peace, and not of evil.*
JEREMIAH 29:11

BELONGING

Belinda hated goodbyes. The tears, the hugs, the promises. She wished there were an easier way to leave. But it was the doubts that made this goodbye most difficult. Belinda had so many doubts—so many worries. She wondered for the hundredth time if she was doing the right thing. When would she be home again? What would bring her back? Some tragedy? She prayed not. But who could tell? Her mother and father were getting older. Belinda shivered at the thought.

Marty held Belinda close as though to protect her from the chill of the wind and the pain of the world.

Clark held her then. She felt his arms tighten about her. She kissed her mother one last time and then, amid shouts of "goodbye," she climbed the train steps and selected a seat. Leaning from the window, she waved one last time. The train was taking her back to Boston. *Back to where I belong,* thought Belinda. *But if that is so,* she asked herself, *why do I feel so empty inside? Why are my cheeks wet with tears? Why do I feel as if I've just been torn away from everything that is solid?*

[84–85]

When we belong to God, the problem of finding
our place in the world is only a temporary one.

*If any man trust to himself that he is Christ's, let him of
himself think this again, that, as he is Christ's, even so are we
Christ's.*

2 CORINTHIANS 10:7

GOD'S SCALES

Each morning Belinda and Aunt Virgie, as the older woman had asked Belinda to call her, studied a Bible lesson together. Belinda watched for any flickers of understanding on the part of her employer. Aunt Virgie listened attentively, and she attended church services regularly. But Belinda felt that the woman did not really understand the significance of the Christian faith. Aunt Virgie believed that if one tried to be good—was more good than evil—then God's scales would tip in the person's favor.

Belinda selected Scriptures dealing with the sacrificial death of the Savior, the need for a personal faith, the glorious hope of heaven because of what Christ Jesus had done on the sinner's behalf. But though the woman looked sincere, each Bible lesson seemed to fall on deaf ears. Belinda thought often of Christ's parable of the seed and the sower. She wondered if Aunt Virgie would ever be "good ground" or if the evil one would always "snatch the seed" away before it had a chance to root and to grow. [93]

The only way to tip God's scales in our favor is to get on the side with Jesus.

Jesus saith unto him, I am the way, the truth, and the life: no man cometh unto the Father, but by me.

JOHN 14:6

OLD-FASHIONED RELIGION

One Sunday morning Belinda left church feeling empty. The sermon seemed so dry and lifeless. *If he only had gone on—told the rest of the story—explained the meaning of it all,* Belinda chaffed. *But he stopped short, leaving his congregation to sort through the whole thing. No wonder they cannot seem to understand the meaning of the Cross.* Belinda felt like crying as she climbed into the carriage for the ride home.

"Wasn't that a wonderful sermon, dear?" asked Aunt Virgie. Her face was shining in a way Belinda had never seen before. Belinda just nodded dumbly.

"I've heard it over and over, but I've never understood the meaning before. This morning it all came to me. Imagine! The Son of God Himself dying in my place. Isn't it *glorious?* I bowed my head right where I sat and thanked Him over and over."

Belinda stared in wonder. Aunt Virgie had gotten what her pastor at home would call "a good dose of old-fashioned religion"—and in the most unlikely place. In her cold, formal city church.   [93–94]

> When we see the least happening, God may be
> doing the most work.
>
> *O the depth of the riches both of the wisdom and knowledge of*
> *God! how unsearchable are his judgments, and his ways past*
> *finding out!*
> ROMANS 11:33

UNCERTAINTY

Windsor summoned Belinda, his face ashen and his voice choked with emotion. "Come quickly," he trembled. "Something is the matter with M'lady."

Belinda sped from the room. "Call the doctor," she flung over her shoulder as she ran. Belinda rushed to the older woman, but when she bent over her, she knew immediately that a doctor would avail nothing. Aunt Virgie was gone. *Oh, God,* she prayed silently, *what do we all do now? How will we manage to go on without her?* Belinda lowered herself to the floor, leaned her head against the bed, and let sorrow consume her. The doctor and Windsor found her there, her body trembling, her face swollen from crying.

Belinda remembered very little about the rest of the day—the rest of the week. She moved as one in a dream—unfeeling, unnoticing, except for the huge, painful emptiness within her. Over and over she asked herself, "What will we all do now?" But there didn't seem to be any immediate answer. [104–105]

When we're uncertain about what to do, waiting
may be the wisest response.
*Wait on the LORD: be of good courage, and he shall strengthen
thine heart: wait, I say, on the LORD.*
PSALM 27:14

UNUSUAL BURDEN

Belinda fled to the coolness of the gardens, her head spinning, her brain dazed. She lowered herself onto a white wrought-iron bench beneath a lilac bush and tried to clear her fuzzy thinking. *This bush was covered with blossoms this spring, but there's nothing here now—nothing. You wouldn't even know it had ever bloomed. Thomas has clipped all the seed pods.*

"How time changes," she whispered. "Seasons come and go— life begins and stops. A person has such a short time to make any impression on the world."

It could have been a morbid thought, but to Belinda it was one of action. It helped her to put things into proper perspective. "I was going home," she said, speaking aloud in the quiet garden. "Had my mind all made up, and now—now I have this house— Marshall Manor—to contend with. I'm trapped. Aunt Virgie didn't intend for it to be a burden—she didn't mean to force me into a difficult circumstance. She thought she was doing me a favor—giving me an honor. But it isn't so. I don't want her house and her money. I stayed because she needed me—and now— now I am still not free to go." [111–112]

> We think that having more possessions will ease
> our burdens, but it's more likely that the
> possessions themselves will become a burden.
> *Take heed, and beware of covetousness: for a man's life
> consisteth not in the abundance of the things which he
> possesseth.*
> LUKE 12:15

RENEWED FRIENDSHIP

*C*an it possibly be? Belinda's heart gave a sudden lurch.

"Drew?"

The man wheeled sharply. "Belinda! Belinda Davis! It *is* you!" he said, shaking his head in wonder. "It really *is* you! I thought I must be dreaming."

"What are you doing here?" Belinda asked.

"I—I work for this firm," he responded. "And you?"

"I've been working in the city for three years," Belinda answered.

"I can't believe it! Here we are—in the same city, so—so close to each other and never knowing it. How about a cup of tea together so we can catch up a bit? I have a few minutes."

"Oh, could we?" Belinda quickly answered. "That would be so nice. I need a friend—someone I can talk to," she said. "I've had too many decisions to make in too short a time."

Drew escorted Belinda to a small tea shop and settled her at a table. "Now," he said, "we don't have nearly enough time, so we will have to talk fast."

Belinda smiled. She no longer felt desperate—or lonely. She was so glad to see someone from home. She was so glad to see Drew.   [147–148]

When an old friend is also a new friend, the
pleasure doubles.

A friend loveth at all times.
PROVERBS 17:17

COMPLICATIONS

Looking about him at the magnificent home, Drew pondered, "Seems a shame to have it all pass on to someone else. Someone who might not love it in the way your employer did."

"That's why I don't want it sold," Belinda agreed.

Drew looked surprised. "I thought you were busy settling the estate."

"Oh, yes. I am, but that's all been taken care of. That wasn't the difficult part. The problem has been setting things up to convert the mansion into a home for the elderly. It's perfectly suited for it. They can live in dignity—with the company of others. They can walk in the gardens, sit in the sunshine. They will have the library, the music room. But there are so many details, and I don't want things to deteriorate. It takes a good deal of planning to maintain such a place."

Drew looked puzzled. "Why do you have to do all of that?" he asked.

"Because Aunt Virgie left it all to me," Belinda responded simply.

Belinda had no idea the effect her words had on Drew. The impact of the simple statement took the wind out of him. Belinda's wealth put an impossible barrier between her and the struggling young attorney.   [168–169]

We think wealth will make life simpler, but it
usually makes it more complicated.
*He that trusteth in his riches shall fall: but the righteous shall
flourish as a branch.*
PROVERBS 11:28

On December 10 three more residents moved into the Manor, making the total five. Mr. Rudgers was a tall, thin man with an untidy mustache and a twinkle in his eyes. Belinda took to him immediately. Mr. Lewis, wizened and bent, had no twinkle in his eyes, only sorrow. Belinda hoped that life in the Manor would soon erase some of his pain. Mrs. Gibbons was wiry and talkative. She fluttered here and there asking questions. With Mrs. Gibbons prompting and prodding, Belinda was sure everyone would be acquainted in no time at all.

Three more guests moved in the week before Christmas. And on December 21, a marvelous thing happened. A retired minister and his wife came to the Manor. Their home had been destroyed by fire and they had no means to rebuild. Belinda sorrowed for their loss, but she felt the couple was God's answer to her prayers. The gentle old man smiled as Belinda asked him about becoming the spiritual director for the residents.

"God be praised, Nettie," he said, addressing his silver-haired helpmate of many years. "He has given us a home *and* a place of service—not a shelf on which to sit." [181–182]

God has a place of service for every person willing to serve.

As every man hath received the gift, even so minister the same one to another, as good stewards of the manifold grace of God.
1 PETER 4:10

UNSELFISHNESS

"Did I tell you the good news?" Belinda asked Drew as she poured his tea. "We have a nurse. That was the last detail to be worked out. I had so hoped to have everything in place by Christmas. And here it is. All set. I can hardly believe it."

"You are really something," Drew said quietly. "Who else would take this beautiful inheritance and share it with a houseful of other people? You are the most unselfish person I've ever met."

"Please," she said, "don't make a saint of me. Aunt Virgie expected me to *use* the house—not just harbor it."

"That's what I love about your family," Drew went on. "You all think life is meant to be shared with others. Unselfishness is as natural as breathing. That was what convinced me there was really something sound about Christianity. I saw faith lived and breathed in the form of your father." [191—192]

Giving to others what is rightfully ours is a good indication that we are following Christ's example.
Give, and it shall be given unto you; good measure, pressed down, and shaken together, and running over, shall men give into your bosom. For with the same measure that ye mete withal it shall be measured to you again.
LUKE 6:38

HAPPY ENDING

Belinda judged it to be the most glorious spring she had ever experienced. She and Drew had both left Boston and returned home, where their love for each other had grown. Marty just smiled at her daughter. She had watched love bloom before.

Drew found a small house on the edge of town and made arrangements to rent it. Belinda spent hours dreaming how she would fix it. "It's going to be just perfect," she kept saying.

Drew smiled. The place certainly wasn't perfect, especially after what Belinda had been used to in Boston. But he no longer worried about asking her to share his dreams. Love was evident on her face, and he knew that they would be happy together.

One day when the sun was spilling its warm promise upon the earth, Belinda headed for her new home with the potted "Princess Belinda" rose Thomas had given her. She placed the small bush tenderly into the ground. "Grow, little rose," she whispered. "I hope you will be happy here. As happy as I intend to be. You are to make our home beautiful on the outside—and I will try to make it beautiful on the inside. I hope you bloom this year, but if you don't—I'll wait. I feel prepared to wait now. I finally feel settled—ready for life." [217–218]

The happiest ending of all is when we are home
with the ones we love and the One who loves us.
Being rooted and grounded in love, may [you] be able to
comprehend . . . the love of Christ . . . that ye might be filled with
all the fulness of God.
EPHESIANS 3:17–19